Fat

New and Uncollected Prose

Also by W. S. Di Piero

Poetry

The First Hour
The Only Dangerous Thing
Early Light
The Dog Star
The Restorers
Shadows Burning
Skirts and Slacks
Brother Fire
Chinese Apples: New and Selected Poems
Nitro Nights
TOMBO
The Complaints

Essays

Memory and Enthusiasm: Essays 1975-1985
Out of Eden: Essays on Modern Art
Shooting the Works: On Poetry and Pictures
City Dog
When Can I See You Again: New Art Writings
Mickey Rourke and the Bluebird of Happiness: A Poet's Notebooks

Translations

Pensieri, Giacomo Leopardi
This Strange Joy: Selected Poems of Sandro Penna
Night of Shooting Stars: The Selected Poems of Leonardo Sinisgalli
Ion, Euripides

Fat

New and Uncollected Prose

W. S. Di Piero

Carnegie Mellon University Press
Pittsburgh 2020

Acknowledgments

The author wishes to thank the editors of the following publications in which these essays first appeared:

New York Review Books Classics: "To Each His Own"
Poetry: "What's for Dinner?," "Fat," "Baby Sweetness Blew His Cool Again," "Brag, Sweet Tenor Bull," "Get Chianti"
Poetry Foundation: "No Blot, Nor Blank"
San Diego Reader: "Sketches of Spain," "Father's Day"
San Francisco Chronicle: "Show It Again"
StoryQuarterly: "On Not Reading Fiction"
The Threepenny Review: "Poor Tom," "Neighborhood," "Who Shot Snot?," "What's for Lunch?"

The following appeared as columns in the *San Diego Reader*: "Renoir's Girls," "Varnishing Days," "Rembrandt All Over," "Sacred Space," "The Writing on the Wall," "The Jazz Loft" "Picture Perfect," "The Great War God," "Ripped," "Exciting Events!"

I've had editors who have acted in good faith and held me upright whenever I started to list. I thank in particular Wendy Lesser, Christian Wiman, and Jim Holman.

Cover art:
Ed Ruscha
Little Snitches Like You End Up in Dumpsters All Across Town, 1997
acrylic on rayon-covered board
20 x 16 inches
©Ed Ruscha, courtesy of the artist and Gagosian

Book design by Connie Amoroso

Library of Congress Control Number 2020943708
ISBN 978-0-88748-662-3

10 9 8 7 6 5 4 3 2 1

for Laura

Contents

Postscript

A Sense of Things

Show It Again

I don't have cable, so the day after the attack on the World Trade Center I depended on radio and local papers for news. A friend admonished that someone like me, a poet who writes about the visual arts, has to *see* what happened, so that evening I walked down to Kezar, my local place, ordered a drink from Jessie, the genial but that night subdued bartender, and looked up at the muted TV monitor. There on the split screen was froggy Larry King, side-barred by a replay of the Boeing 767 spearing into the World Trade Center South Tower while the North Tower fumed. Then the fireball. Then panicked New Yorkers running and fire crews at work. Then the implosion of both buildings, the chunky meltdown and foaming smoke.

As the video loop played over and over, the guy next to me tucked into his cheeseburger and fries while reading newspaper coverage, occasionally looking up at imagery he had already seen now many times. Neither TV nor newspaper put him off his food. I finished my drink and got out of there. I'm no sensitive plant, no more or less sensitive than Mr. Burger-and-Fries, but enough is enough.

But when is enough really enough? How much repetition of horror suffices? And to what end? In the short while I watched that footage, its images were already turning into clichés, visual commentary repeated like numbed prayer as a charm against oblivion, forgetfulness, or the dulling of the senses, even though cliché, if it does nothing else, dulls the senses. Our feeble vocabulary of the horrific—"terrible human tragedy," "unprecedented heinous act," "day of infamy"—becomes a compendium of commonplaces. We repeat, the *culture* repeats, certain phrases and pictures to heighten the reality of the event so that we continue to experience its force. And the more they're repeated, the more unreal the event becomes. The more it becomes—here's another commonplace—like a movie. It *is* a movie, that video loop, it's just not fiction, though like a theatrical movie the event was scrupulously casted and staged, down to the grotesque joke of the 9-11 date. In any case, such barroom images soon become a hermetically sealed memory. The imagination can't add to or detract from them—just like a movie. When America retaliates, we'll need, maybe crave, an equal tonnage of visuals as a vindictive moral counterweight.

The diluvial commentary by the media and amongst ourselves (like everyone else, I needed to discuss the event with loved ones and strangers) is crucial: if we stop talking about it, the event would silence us all. Words give some primitive shape to the disordering forces of what happened and help consciousness accommodate it. Our words are meant to master what would otherwise master us, even while what we continue to say is that words can't describe, can't master, the enormity of the reality. Hannah Arendt once wrote that we humanize the world not by living in it but by talking about it. I'd add that it's how we restore the world to ourselves and ourselves to the world.

But talk can be noxious. In an essay on *Uncle Tom's Cabin* James Baldwin says that the sentimentalist is one who possesses "an arid heart," who appropriates others' troubles in order to experience authentic feeling. A San Franciscan on a radio call-in show described how he sobbed in the shower the morning the towers came down, how his tears ran with the shampoo he was rinsing from his hair. That kind of maudlin self-absorption insults the reality of the event. And yet one understands why the talking must go on, even if it concludes in truisms, nostrums, deadbeat verbiage. The suddenly shared recognition of life's fragility and passing-ness, along with the nausea and sickness of heart felt by an entire population unused to public mourning, compel us to speak the word "tragedy" a hundred times, even until it numbs us to the originating bite of the real.

Endless, necessary, feckless but essential verbiage. We're creatures built of words who build images. The Poet Laureate, when asked how poetry can help in the crisis, offered a wilted commonplace, William Butler Yeats's poem "On Being Asked for a War Poem:" "I think it better that in times like these / A poet's mouth be silent, for in truth / We have no gift to set a statesman right: / He has had enough of meddling who can please / A young girl in the indolence of her youth, / Or an old man upon a winter's night." Some of us poets don't agree with Yeats, and it's unfortunate that the Laureate would propagate canned notions. Silence, especially from poets, can be toxic.

But how to break or transcend patterns of repetition which, however much we need them now, will result in verbal and pictorial catatonia? One course, maybe, is to meditate on the awful Luciferian beauty of the image of a plane aimed at a skyscraper by human beings intent on killing as many other human beings as possible, in the inseparable names of God and Politics, until meditation dissolves cliché and yields some meaning beyond the plain horrificness of the event.

2001

Poor Tom

Words are enchantments and dominions. Even numb, blowaway verbal debris knits us more tightly into the weave of our experience. Words give formidable, unyielding shape to certain pieces of our life. Poets aspire to create such shapes. The sounds of poetry enact emotional and intellectual ardor that can recapitulate shockingly raw, fresh states of feeling long after the occasioning event. Words are abundances and afflictions—they give to us and take from us, they're pleasure-givers and pain-bearers. They sing back at us not just knowledge of a singular moment but of an entire historic surround. Poetry makes a memorable impress not because it's precious but because its actions are an impassioned activity of consciousness, and the actions change on us as we grow older. It's a scarily private experience, it's all personal, yet it's only words in sequences.

I had a friend long ago who has lived in my heart mostly as nests and root systems of words, not his but Shakespeare's. The neurogram of his being and the entire nervous system of a particular time in our lives are mapped out in bits and fragments from one play in particular. Bobby B. and I were the same college age, young not-quite-men bored by schoolroom learning but eager for experiential *stuff*, especially the stuff of language. Outside class, we wrote poems and read plays by Marlowe, Shakespeare, Yeats, Eliot. (Do poets still read Yeats's and Eliot's dramatic writings, or have these gone the way of Yeats's powerful *Autobiographies*?) There were no creative writing courses at Saint Joseph's, our Jesuit streetcar college, but we talked endlessly about what we read and wrote and aspired to write. Bobby obsessed over Bob Dylan's meters, I over Hart Crane's meanings. He fussed too much; his repetitive and nearly irrational analytics of Dylan's rhythms reminded me of drawings by outsider artists—meticulously fanatical repetitions of patterns. We both found a provisional shape for our messy obsession with words, and for the jangly blood-energies of our age, by acting in plays. There was no real theater program, no formal training, no schooling in stage performance, except for suggestions from this or that director about intonation, projection, characterization.

At some point, Shakespeare's language, the sounds and move-ments of it, colonized my consciousness, though I couldn't know this at the time. The swimming, hypnagogic imagery that the plays effortlessly (it seemed) spun out, became more and more the rhythms of my inner life, or so it felt. Shakespeare's language became code for a young man's aspirational urgencies. I couldn't get enough of it. I spent a lot of time at rehearsals. Even if I had a picayune role, I'd hang around offstage listening to Richard III or Oberon or Macbeth plot and pilot their conspiracies. I mem-orized chunks of other, lesser parts just by the exposure. It was an irrational thrill: I was internalizing the rush of the dynamics Shakespeare was constantly testing out, the brutal speed-pause-speed of *Macbeth*, the anticipations and surges of *Julius Caesar*, the jumpy wit and articulated moans of *As You Like It*.

One year our little college company performed *King Lear*. After many performances, queasy with an emotional and physical exhaustion we'd never known, Bobby B. and I both got sick with different but equally mystifying illnesses. But that came later. In *Lear* we had matching roles: he, Edgar, runaway pariah prince betrayed by his half-brother; I, the Fool, the nettles-and-honey entertainer who picks apart Lear's moral enfeeblement as well as the operatic hypocrisies of Goneril and Regan, those opportunistic word-mechanics. In a space so noisy with their and Lear's ego-tisms, young Cordelia verbally blanks out. She can only speak that she cannot speak. Her sisters are (like Edgar's brother, Edmond) arch-devaluers of words. When B. and I played the heath scenes, the surround felt like a danger zone. Mania and insanity, real and faked, ruled. That we were amateurs was no safeguard against emotional dissolution and confusion. Precisely because we had no stage training, we had no self-aware emotional governors. Edgar and the Fool are the phi-losophers of divisiveness in the play. Edgar erases himself—"Edgar I nothing am"—and as Tom o' Bedlam takes the enchantments of rational language and cannily maddens and infuriates them: his language becomes a rapture of unreason, turns inside out the structures of clear sense, mocks the carefully worded betrayals and conspiracies other characters live by. He's the poet of the divided mind, riven coherence, scrambled wits. His playacting is too con-vincing: his intimate invocations of devils sound like secrets he has nursed and fed upon. "The Prince of Darkness is a gentleman; Modo he's called, and Mahu." Just so, the Fool taunts his King about rendings, divisions, eggs cracked into two crowns ("with nothing left i' the middle."). The brokenness, the Fool insists, is in his mind: Lear is crack-brained. Edgar's language is a sorcery of summonses. As the earnest, dignified Edgar who turns himself into an unholy fool, he's the most fearless character in the play. As Mad Tom, he's the over-the-edge adjudicater of pity. The Fool, Tom's rival for the king's attention, is the canny lyricist and life-critic who disappears from the play after his encounter with Tom, who becomes Lear's "philosopher."

I was a physical actor and loved roles requiring dancing, sword fights, roughhousing, and other sorts of throw-around mayhem. Bobby was athletic but more cerebral and interiorized, alarmingly so: he had a fearlessness about confronting the worst passages of the inner life. He would utter cryptic things, with a snicker, like "Forgive God." On stage it was a little horrifying to witness his transformation to Mad Tom, whose madness he communicated by cherishing and fondling those diabolical invocations. He was lost to the role of Edgar-Lost-To-Himself. I have no reasonable explanation for the sensation—a compound of hilarity, ecstasy, abandon, mournfulness—aroused in me then and now, so many years later, even in this instant of recording it here, when Mad Tom snaps back to Lear's line, "'Twas this flesh begot // Those pelican daughters," with "Pillicock sat on Pillicock hill: Alow, alow, loo, loo." B. voiced that savage hooting like an animal in distress, then later announced his torment: "The foul fiend bites my back." It was all personal.

Our friends and fellow performers, I learned, thought the two of us were, in our different ways, indestructible and dauntless. We weren't. There was a grotesque, slamming symmetry to what then happened. Not long after we worked in a very different stage world, playing oafish roustabouts in the musical *Carnival*, my body turned on me and I developed mysterious lower body pain that crippled me and put me in the hospital for three months. When Bobby visited me there, he seemed very off, bitterly disoriented about everything he was thinking or doing: he was obsessed with the holocaust and *Crime and Punishment* and was convinced that playing Edgar had permanently damaged him. Not long after his visit I heard his father had had him committed and given shock treatments. In the 1960s shock therapy wasn't as finely calibrated as it now is. The treatments tranquillized his soul but corrupted his fabulous memory. As Edgar, willing himself into a convincing counterfeit of insanity, he'd announced how he would grime his face with filth, "Blanket my loins, elf all my hair in knots, / And with presented nakedness outface / The winds and persecutions of the sky."

Bobby, to me, had virtually turned into a language, so deeply had Shakespeare's words rubbed themselves into the grain of his being. I saw him once more, months after his treatment. I was still semi-disabled; he looked becalmed but not entirely present, like something crudely broken off from time. He gave me a copy of New Directions' just-published edition of the complete *Cantos*, that epic of splintered discontinuities, with a long, baroque inscription that covered the flyleaf and spoke of hope that out of the "dregs" of recent years we'd known together "there may issue something of consequence . . . maybe something not as all-consuming as we might wish it to be but, nevertheless, something."

That was B.'s revised, personalized version of what the restored Edgar says at the end of the play: "We that are young / Shall never see so much, nor live so long." His pre-treatment speech, the intense tonal arcs and dips that made for a sustaining medium of our friendship, now sounded indolent and monotonal. He didn't want to talk about poetry or music or girls. His laughter had always sounded pinched by inner pain, but now he was laughing more than usual. He was working in a men's clothing store, which he thought would be his career. He said that his mind felt a lot calmer after the treatments but that his memory was "completely, ha-ha, *shot*." That year, 1970, was the last I saw or heard from him. He died in 2015. In my head he's Bobby-the-real who is Bobby-the-words: "Bless thy five wits! Tom's a-cold. O do de, do de, do de. Bless thee from whirlwinds, starblasting, and taking! Do poor Tom some charity, whom the foul fiend vexes."

2017

Neighborhood

In Hardy's "The Self-Unseeing" he visits the remains of his child-hood home and recalls where the door was, how the floor felt, how his mother sat "staring into the fire" while her fiddler husband "bowed it higher and higher." The last two bittersweet lines, "Everything glowed with a gleam / Yet we were looking away," remind him they couldn't possibly have been aware of the harmonious moment while living it. They were oblivious, happily so. The moment is what the poem tries to catch up on. We're always late for consciousness, neuroscientists says. And there are durations and degrees of lateness. When conversations turn to the trials of keeping up with the accelerated present, I say I'm still trying to keep up with the past.

If you grow up in a concentrated, tribal, old-style, working-class neighborhood, as I did, you're in the dream and can't see it, conceptualize it, or even short-term remember it, as you eventually will in time. It's a mossy nutrient medium and you're the bacterial culture growing in it. You don't control much. I spent more or less the first twenty-one years of my life in an insular, red-brick, South Philadelphia neighborhood, a village really, unaware how the place, its physical and emotional climate, was saturating my consciousness. The surround (voices, odors, sounds: the givella-water man shouting his arrival, the fresh manure hot from his horse, the rocking tock-tock of his wagon—this was the 1950s) composed, and in my head continues to dilate, an entity greater than all of its pieces. But I was oblivious to what was forming me and modeling my mentality.

To outsiders, a neighborhood is mostly local color. Live there, though, and local color is your life, invisible to you. When I finally moved away, my neighborhood, where there were no gardens, became a subject in my garden of writing: something was always growing or dying there. I think of it as the Matter of South Philadelphia (as one speaks of the Matter of Britain): it can't be my property because it doesn't belong to me, it *is* me. To honor my own looking away, I act in good faith to the material by reimagining it: the reimagination of the place is a preservative and maybe, maybe, makes me a little less late for consciousness.

I've now lived in San Francisco, in the same apartment in the Upper Haight, for twenty years. The surround has been stitching itself to my being, I'm sure, though it's not the First Place that South Philadelphia was. It's more a set of clothes I wear, baggy or too tight, silky or itchy. The difference is the consciousness, the seeing—of the self, the ambience, the dynamic that's engaged when I'm being witness to what I'm already a part of. I'm less late for consciousness but still prickly about local color. It calls attention to itself, it fondles too cozily the details of neighborhood life, it craves to be admired or adored. Local color doesn't disclose value or inquire into value. It's mostly a collection of icons. It estranges poets from their material and becomes the kind of irony that baffles revelation.

I spent several years in a neighborhood on the Peninsula south of San Francisco that I never felt to be my neighborhood. The "my" matters. Everyone around me referred to the place as the "neighborhood." Let me back up. I lived for three years in the historic center of Bologna, next to the old Jewish ghetto that was also once the red light district. It was a neighborhood, like any neighborhood worth the name, with sensual textures and definitions that became memorable even while I was inhabiting them. A neighborhood requires sidewalk velocities (which require pedestrians), daily noise (or streetside sound design) particular to the place, and people greeting others. I'm *still* not looking away from Bologna. It's also different from other places I've lived because of its historical strata, down through the Middle Ages and Dante to the Romans and Etruscans. My neighborhood was antiquity. You hear visitors speak of Bologna as elegant, friendly, sophisticated. My birthplace, on the other hand, is of a kind that people who have never actually experienced it like to call gritty, colorful, *real*. In its raw ways, it's enchantingly *other* for everybody except us. And yet in 1950s and 1960s South Philadelphia everybody owned a house and car: it was, still is, nudged along by the razor-fingered American Dream. Eventually it created in me a comic, contrary, perverse consciousness: in order to feel like I'm living in a real neighborhood now, I can't own a house or car, have a driveway or a dishwasher. This, I admit, is creepy, autocratic, and precious.

But back to my overcast times in an exceedingly bright place. For six years I owned a house, the only one I've owned, in Redwood City, California, which I never felt to be my neighborhood, whatever my property rights. Though it must have been *a* neighborhood. My neighbors called it so. There were no redwood trees in sight. It couldn't possibly be a neighborhood (I felt) because outsiders would find no local color there and I couldn't feel any palpable textures. It reinforced my sense of what a working neighborhood has: easily available public transport, walking distance to markets, hardware stores, eating places, cafés, nail salons and hair salons, saloons, dry cleaners, laundromats, and an ongoing itemizable list of casual personal infrastructure. Redwood City had a few strip malls and a shopping center, as suburbs do, so it could never be my kind of neighborhood. It may have been nutrient-rich for my neighbors, who were mostly working-class people in the building trades, landscaping, and law enforcement, but I was a sickly failing culture in it.

What is the suburban? A physical (and moral) locale where

the entity of the space doesn't have a life greater than the lives of its inhabitants. It lacks grace. It's not a culture of wealth so much as one of markers, icons, large garages, lawns, citizens who prefer taking walks to walking. The flâneur, the idea of the flâneur, is existentially irrelevant, though there are many friendly looking dogs, outdoor grills, and a profound observance of quietude. Not city, not country. A neighborhood, like the San Francisco one I'm in now, is defined by the body, mine, moving through space shared with other bodies, with signature styles of dress, gait, smell. A neighborhood is a measure of individual and group capacities, of what the body can do—walk, shop, meet and converse with strangers; get on and off and in and out of streetcars, buses, Ubers, cabs; and occasionally witness or intervene in a street ruckus, though the Haight isn't classically self-policed the way South Philadelphia was, where no man on my street owned a gun but all had baseball bats by the front door in case of unrest amongst street villains or public women-bashers. My own experience is only what it is, it's not representative; but I'm still catching up on understanding why I never felt at home in the neighborhood where I lived in the only house I've ever owned.

2017

Sketches of Spain

I've been sleeping on a lumpy sofa for several days, and my back is on fire. The sofa isn't in my own house, a take-no-prisoners zone I return to only to collect fresh clothes, but in the house of elderly friends kind enough to shelter me. It's 1967, I'm twenty-two, I've lived in South Philadelphia all my days and graduated from a local college where I lost a year because of a crippling inflammatory condition called ankylosing spondylitis that put me in the hospital for months, left me slow and gimpy, and made my lower back a kiln that fires up whenever I sleep on that sofa.

For months, life's details, each and every one, have felt intractable or inscrutable. To get by, I work a series of noble jobs: insurance company file clerk; mail sorter at Oscar Mayer Wiener; bookstore cashier. My safe house is here, in my friends' high-ceilinged airy rooms, scented with bayberry candles and fresh-cut lilacs, in a hamlet outside a town with the winning Welsh name of Gwynedd Valley. But then, I'm also in love with the two daughters of the house, and they with me. We manage assignations at different times, sometimes on the same day, with no one any the wiser, we think.

One kind of mental breakdown is caused by the impacting of the minutest details of everyday life into each separate instant. It's not overload, exactly, so much as a feeling that the body, already too head-heavy, is filling with concrete that while it begins to set also begins to crack from amassed internal pressure. The heaviest concentration and most groaning crack is the sacral lumbar pain that keeps me awake most nights on the sofa, across from which is a window that lets in silky evening breezes; on an oak table before the window sits a turntable. One night, I play a record I've just acquired and have, as they say, a moment.

◎◎◎

It's now 2005, and the vinyl beauty I spun that night, along with all my other sides, got sold off several months later with practically everything else I owned—clothes, books, turntable, speakers, and a beloved Webcor reel-to-reel tape deck that mysteriously fell into my hands after it fell off a truck—so that I could launch myself from Philadelphia to land's end in San Francisco. I now own that album on CD and listen to it every so often, not to remind myself of that other time of my life (though of course it does that, too) but to set free a mysterious force that cuts right through me with a pleasure threaded with vague menace.

The opening bars of *Sketches of Spain*, one of the three albums Gil Evans arranged for Miles Davis backed by a large ensemble, punch me into a peculiarly heightened wakefulness. (The track is a reworking of Joaquin Rodrigo's composition for guitar and orchestra, *Concierto de Aranjuez*.) Nothing on the other two Evans-Davis collaborations have quite this effect, not the lush grievousness of *Porgy and Bess* or the sky-clearing arousals of *Miles Ahead*, my personal favorite. The Evans-Davis *Concierto* begins with faint castanet cricketing. Then the silence splits open with a flute and brass brilliantined with wariness, a slightly dissonant reedy reveille of consciousness, a call. It's bold, but it trembles. It has a Romantic rawness; its ringing tones *are* the bayberry, the lumpiness, and the sisters' very different fragrances; it also carries a piercing sensation of life's beautiful unforgiving totality. Other choice passages throughout the recording have the same effect. They bite into my bones a bereaved cry. But what, exactly, has been lost?

2005

Father's Day

The voices of the dead, when I hear or think I'm hearing them, sometimes thrum in my head like hundreds of bees I once heard in a blossoming almond tree. Other times they are the mariachi tunes or cabbies' chatter in telephone static, or party noise from the apartment downstairs. Among them is the voice of a combative old friend of mine, a translator and critic, who had two daughters, no sons, and who welcomed surrogate student-sons into his life, but only if they were willing to contend with him. He could only love those willing to fight him. His intellectual hero and father was Nietzsche, who never wanted to father anything except contentious thoughts and who said that the truly great teachers are those who teach their students to kill their teachers.

Then there's the sound made by a man from the Italian neighborhood where I grew up, whom all the women thought the kindest male in a community not known for male kindness. He had two sons, one daughter, and was once accused of sexual predation by an eighth grade girl he was only trying to console (he said) after her father died. And there's the snoring noise coming from one of my uncles, the only Jew in the family, who had two daughters, no sons, and was the favorite of all the boys because of his standard surly greeting: "Hey, knucklehead, you're as ugly as your old man. How'd you get so ugly?" That fake belligerence seemed more loaded with affection, all the more for its fake belligerence, than anything our fathers said. He was the only man in the family who could cook—exotic fare like borscht, roast duck, and potato latkes—and he cooked better than the women. He had narcolepsy and once nearly got himself killed when he fell asleep at the wheel with his beloved Shih Tzu, Happy, in his lap.

My father's voice is mixed in with them. Husky vowels, that's how I recognize him. Because he died when I was a teenager I have sufficient salient memories to identify him as a person but not nearly enough to create that historically matured, conscious-ness-shaped condition which is understanding. My memories of him are broken incomplete chunks of experience. I can hear his heavy, child-like, step-by-step way of going up and down stairs because of his fused knee, the result of a war wound. I hear his embarrassed laugh, as if he were shamed by his own laughter, but I have no memory of him smiling at me.

He drank and died from it. At his hospital bedside nearly every day, I watched the body bloat with fluids, shrivel when drained (my clearest image the puncture wound in his gut) then inflate again. He was a simple man, or maybe I think so only because we never really had conversations, so I can fantasticate any qualities I like. I do know he was melancholic and psychologically fragile in ways that the culture refused to acknowledge as anything other than unmanly inadequacy. When I see expressions of love between fathers and sons on the street, in the movies, at the opera, wherever, I'm devastated, even in middle age, and lost. He loved me, I'm certain of that, though I don't remember any expression of it except in unspoken, oblique ways. In the summer of 1959, he took me to a drive-in to see Gregory Peck in *Pork Chop Hill*. It was raining hard. His heavy presence, the envelope of rain and car, the tinny intimacy of the sound box, they made me feel safe—just about the only time I ever felt so—and I experienced that momentary safety as love. Another time, driving home from the American Legion post where he liked to drink, he told funny stories about basic training, such as the time he dug a trench incorrectly around his tent, which consequently flooded while he slept. He was tipsy and laughed out loud.

On a night I couldn't sit with him, he died, and this has since given shape to my most frequent dream. I'm in a strange house. An awareness comes to me: to my sorrow and horror, he's actually been alive all these years, ill and alone in a vague somewhere (often upstairs hidden away in a room I didn't know existed) and I've let pass all this time we might have spent together. Maybe a dream of unrealized or withheld understanding. But the feeling tone overwhelms explanation. It's not just the pain of loss, it's the despair of knowing I might have done something about it, because stirred into the dream is the shame of recognition: having sworn never to forget him, I've forgotten. In the dream he's speechless. He speaks to me, in sounds I can't understand, only when I'm awake and hearing the voices of all those other fathers.

2004

Desire

I've been reading the *Henry IV* plays and thinking about appetite, aspiration, and desire. Falstaff's colossal appetites, all that sack and whoring and food, are instinct amplified to comically catastrophic wont. Desire is too abstract for him, though in his Falstaffian way he does aspire to certain things: he wants social and political distinction, and a comfortable retirement. His aspirations are weaponized by cowardice. The most comically horrifying act in Shakespeare occurs on the fields of Shrewsbury: first Falstaff feigns death to avoid getting killed, then when he comes across the truly dead Hotspur—"Mars in swathling clothes, / This infant warrior," King Henry calls him—he sticks his sword into the corpse and claims the kill.

Appetite and aspiration are children of the will, desire the child of the imagination. Appetite is pure existential agency, a force driving us to acquire something and satiate ourselves. Falstaff's compelling aspiration, one that in his heart he knows can't be realized, is to become Prince Hal's Prime Minister. Aspiration is yeasty with hope. Appetite doesn't need hope; it bypasses sensibility, deliberation. Desire is more deliberative and discriminating and yet makes us mad. To our woe or glory, it makes us feverish to think about what's not even there. It's inflected by the absence of the object, by impossibility, by love: we desire what we already know we cannot have, and desire tells us we can lose things we've never had. It doesn't just consume what's there, as appetite does, because there's nothing before it. Desire thrives on distance, remoteness, ineluctability. We experience it as obsessively singular. It's a soul climate that kidnaps agency even while it's ruled by the intensest subjectivity.

Falstaff is so compelled by appetite and gross aspiration that something he says late in the play, even in its casual utterance, stops me: he's rehearsing his appearance before his new King and says he is "sweating with desire to see him, thinking of nothing else." Just so. Desire colonizes us. It's typical of Falstaff to express desire's ardent atmospheres in terms of the sweating, agued, snotty body. Appetite's motor drives the body's demands. Desire, though we speak of its having objects, is really a wrap or medium that, when desire is most autocratic, turns reality, every bit of it, into a hall of mirrors reflecting something else as an aspect or avatar of itself, some absence, not even in the room. We experience its ardor, but also, maybe most of all, its stupefaction. It's a weird music—*wyrd* music, dulcet or dissonant—and inescapable, a state we can't be delivered from.

Desire wants what the imagination wants: to be complete, to realize completeness. If appetite is a force and aspiration a leaning-into, desire is a constant haunter: we feel its acuity and neediness even if we can't discern its object. It causes us to ache or agonize over what we already know to be unattainable. It empowers us to miss dreadfully what we've never actually possessed. It's a pain and an ecstasy. It's the condition our condition is in.

2019

What's for Dinner?

Two tables over, in a sushi joint in my San Francisco neighborhood, I see a young couple cozied next to each other and think of the great blue heron I'd watched in Tomales Bay. I didn't see it at first because of its stillness, still in a way human animals never seem still: its entire body was an instrument of seeing, its length an embodiment of casually dire attentiveness. The heron was hunting, waiting for some bite-sized thing to forget it was there. It stretched and retracted its neck a couple of times in that elastic-cable way they have, went still again for a long time, ten minutes maybe—I know because silly, top-of-the-line mammal me tried to stay as still as the bird—then snapped its head into the rushes, and when it came back into sight, a furry thing wriggled in its beak, but only for a few mortal moments. In the restaurant, the woman feeding had a similar rhythm: she reached chopsticks tentatively toward her and her man's shared sashimi plate, then withdrew them, as if anticipating the perfect moment. After a few tentative gestures, she stabbed at the plate, clamped a slice of flesh, retrieved it to her lips, took a tiny bite, and chewed. I couldn't hear their conversation, though I did hear from her a squeak that in another venue would have passed for orgasmic utterance. She beaked the remaining chunk of fish into her mouth, bit down on it, chewed once, twice, then did something I've never seen: as some animals feed their young with prey they've caught and chewed, tipping the macerated remains into the younger mouths or beaks, she turned and, covering mouth and chopstick tips with her hand, retrieved that last chewed morsel from her mouth and placed it into her mate's astonished, hesitant mouth, and they masticated together, nodding. The scene reminded me of a conversation I'd had with a friend who had just broken up with her fiancée. "I couldn't stand it. The way he put his head down like a dog to a dish and snorted his food, it disgusted me. Feeding time in the lion house or pigpen. We're all animals, sure, and he was an animal in bed, which was okay, but slurping pho and squishing ahi like that? That was a deal-breaker."

Physical taste, like one's sense of style, is fixed, foundational, irreducible. Science will someday map and analyze neural networks sufficiently to explain all this, but for now it remains a mystery to me. Taste is radical, it roots us in the world, to our sense of our presence in reality. It's foundational but radiates something restless and migratory. It radiates imagination: once we've tasted something that strikes deeper than any other sensation into a darker, more obscure part of consciousness, we may spend the rest of our existence trying to replicate the experience, or hoping without hope that it will incidentally replicate itself. I was eight or nine maybe when my grandmother first offered me a slice of fresh fennel. The anise sweetness, its toothy cool striated texture, ripped it out of the crowded neighborhood of like flavors I already knew—licorice whips, anisette, Good & Plenty—and, liberating itself, liberated me, or my completeness of sensational pleasure, to seek it out again, and I have, and I like the taste still but that first taste was like an adamic act of naming a piece of reality. You only do it once. I've written poems that revisit the experience, but that's all that poetry can do, revisit, not remake or even intensify it, because my primary experience was already the intensest rendezvous. One agony of the imagination is that it returns us again and again to the recognition that there is no earthly paradise, though we're sickeningly equipped to imagine one. I've chased that primal savoriness ever since. Desire drives imagination but doesn't empower it. Our nagging desire to experience a taste afresh reminds us that that acquisition was really a loss of innocence, and once lost, any recovery is an illusion or willed fabrication.

◉◉◉

Innate distaste drives a contrary desire—to pursue and conquer a taste that resists us, to claim and colonize it, even though you disapprove of and find inferior the new colony's native inhabitants and culture and forms of religious worship. My two food missions— marshmallows and orange things—are driven, in other words, by perverted desire. My success rate stinks. Marshmallow (*Althea officinalis*) is an herb usually found near wetlands whose leaves and roots have been used since ancient Egypt as a simple for ailments ranging from asthma to agita to cankers. But that's not what comes in those respiratory plastic bags or in S'mores. For me, as a child, marshmallows were the anti-fennel, a sickening vaporous sweetness hugging stringy foamed-over nothingness. Kissing cousin to cotton candy. (On the boardwalk, give me a hoagie or bag of warm peanuts, pass the cotton candy to the girlfriend.) The mini marshmallows I confronted as an adult, in the Midwest, in Jell-O salad, were contaminants. Jell-O was devious joker food, a shapeshifter, now a solid, now liquefied on the tongue, mostly something slitheringly in between, and it was colored Green Hornet emerald, Captain Marvel carmeline, or Aquaman cyan. Who could ask for more? But those scrawny pasty cubes? I ate around them and left a gummy, mucilaginous refuse in the bowl. And yet I had a dream of deliverance: on TV, where perfect experience was had by perfect people I knew must exist in a faraway land, jolly clans toasted marshmallows over a fire. Campfire, fireplace, no matter. Fire's fire. But since it never occurred to us to roast those foamy virgin organs over a stovetop flame, I waited many years before the opportunity offered itself. The charred caramelized sheath, the steamy inner goop—the mighty thing itself that would redeem me from my un-American disgust—pitched my disgust beyond mere disgust.

And spare me two orange foods, yams and pumpkin pie. I'm not a hater of All-American ceremonial foods (in my culture, Thanksgiving turkey and its infinite fixings were preceded by industrial-strength raviolis tanked in estuarial red gravy) but gagging on my first mouthful of pumpkin pie at some childhood holiday dinner seemed to grievously violate a pact of conscience with our Sea-to-Shining-Sea. That was predetermined, I should have known, by the bite of yam I'd stupidly eaten (nobody warned me) and which I cleverly excused myself from table to cough back into the toilet, much as certain animals cough up food to nourish their young, yes? But unlike the fake leaf-and-root extract from marshy lands that had permanently become a species alien to my gut, from my aversion toward orange foods I *was* finally delivered (thanks to the culinary cunning of women who couldn't have known they held my destiny and desire in their hands) by a critical additive to both yams and the odious Rupert Pupkin bupkis pup-poop pumpkin pie.

> *Cognac.*
>> *Cognac.*

So I bless Bacchus, nemesis of bupkis, I bless the grape, O galvanic grape and all your ministrations, and your mutations, and let me also bless the grappa of the grape and Pavese's poem, "Grappa in September," for you have all made me the man I am today.

2011

Who Shot Snot?

This is sticky. If you haven't watched all five seasons of *The Wire,* what follows might sound encrypted. I can't unpack its plots because it would be like unpacking *Bleak House.* The names, events, and dialogue textured into over a dozen cannily inflected storylines, the tight yet elastic weave of relations among characters from very different orders of society, the lingos and temperaments and mayhem and everything else that figure in a sixty-hour master story that's pure process, without an originating event or conclusion: these are by now a language shared by *Wire* initiates. I'll presume that if you read on, you know or are soon to know what's what. If you're a noninitiate, know that spoilers follow.

I don't have cable service but I have a TV set, so I catch up to things on DVD. When I caught *The Wire,* I watched every season as it was released, back-to-back episodes, sometimes three a night. I couldn't let it go; it wouldn't let me go. I told anyone who asked that it was the best television I'd ever seen. I never tried to figure out why until I decided to write about it. I'm still figuring it out, so this is a provisional report on what keeps me hooked.

I'm watching it for the third time and am hearing and seeing bits I missed the first two times around because of the show's rarest pleasure—its elliptical narrative tactics and speed. Storylines pitch forward while withholding crucial information, and the withholding is technique *and* content. Stutter-step disclosures drive the show's narrative and incidentally allow me to delight in my own information deprivation. Every plot line is about late arrivals at momentous recognitions which, when they do finally come, are dumped like asides, ticked past with herky-jerky indifference, or allowed to die a slightly double-take death.

The Wire has the conventional dynamics of cops-and-robbers shows: double crosses, tough talk, bleak comedy, gals rough and sweet (or both), moral ambiguities, and gun-play. And I do love all that. But it's also about storytelling, how we represent experience and craft our separate realities, how we control the lives of others by eliding or withholding disclosures. Season one begins with a story being told, and the final, fifth season is about the mass storytelling—misleading, self-interested, redacted—of newspapers.

So, episode one, scene one. Visuals unceremoniously drop us into an in-progress event: wet blood-tracks on a street, then a teenage male corpse leaking that blood, then a beat cop writing his report, all impassively watched by young children and by a detective, Jimmy McNulty, later referred to as "McNutty" by Bubbs, a sweet-natured junkie informant whose street name is Bubbles and whose birth name (we learn many hours later) is Reginald. The sliding scale of names is part of the mechanics of unknowing and misdirection that sustain *The Wire*, and no story reported by any character to another—like any story picked up off the wire—can be entirely trusted. McNulty, the Greek, the Mayor of Baltimore, the small-appliance-repairman-cum-drug-lord Prop Joe, Senator Clay Davis, Stringer Bell, Bunk, D'Angelo, the Sibotkas, Brother Mouzone and Omar and Cheese and Wee-Bey and Pook and others with such inventive names represent reality to each other with the same blind spots and obliquities that the show uses. *The Wire* opens up "story arcs" in fractured, askance ways, just as McNutty occludes virtually all the information he passes on to his police superiors, his wife, his hook-ups, his kids, whoever. The stories are about characters orienting themselves to constantly morphing circumstances, and we viewers are deposited into disorientation with them. *The Wire* is organized so that pieces and fragments of information get pinned to our prepped story-telling grid like the index cards and photos pinned to the cops' big storyboard: it gives us the big picture of why no big picture is ever completed.

But back to the opening scene. A project mook sitting with McNulty narrates the back-story. Snot, the dead kid's street name, shoots craps every Friday with his boys and, every time, when the pot gets deep, he scoops up the money and runs and his boys catch him and rough him up. It happens every Friday, until tonight, when disorder stepped in and Snot got shot. When McNutty asks the kid why, since everybody knew Snot (full name Snot Boogie) grabbed the pot every time, they let him play at all, the kid answers: "You gots to. This America, man." The glum, throwaway remark gives momentary if obtuse moral coherence to messy street life.

The messiness and the abrupt revising or finalizing of desti-nies, as the series plays out, extends to other chunks of the social order: law enforcement, the drug trade, labor unions, City Hall, schools, media. And yet every setting has an infrastructure for provisional stability. For drug players it's the Game. If you're in it, you abide by an ethos of authoritarian rules that determine how business gets transacted, rules more often assumed than stated. The Game allows for a disrupter, the murderous prankster Omar, whose "work" is taking down drug stashes and who relishes the Game more shamelessly than anyone. (The projects know he's coming when they hear him whistling an ain't-I-ironic version of "Farmer in the Dell.") As in any secret society, those in the Game recognize those who aren't, or who want to leave or are unsuited to it. When D'Angelo's agonized sense of right and wrong begins to override the Game's precepts—this is a young man who hasn't just committed murder but who compellingly *narrates* it, like a project bard, to his pals—he's executed on the orders of his own beloved mentor, String. It's D' who recognizes that the baby-faced Wal-lace isn't cut out for the Game. The show is so cannily inflected, though, that when D' tells his story and stops short of the punch line, the kid who supplies it—"He shot her"—is Wallace, a boy soon so appalled and addled by the violence he's witnessed that he takes to bed, depressed. He can't man up anymore, wants out of the Game, and so is suspect, and so he, too, is killed (by two of his own boys) in the most agonizing act of violence in the entire series.

In law enforcement (another secret society) the Game becomes Chain of Command, in stevedores' lives it's Union, in the political order it's City Hall, and the leering mistrust in each runs so deep that the actors often look like they're inhaling some rotten odor. Season to season, we see each society conniving to maintain an ethos, however twisted or opportunistic, that will forestall chaos. The show's mechanics imitate its contents: it uses correspondences between social orders (cut from an elementary-school soccer match to project kids aimlessly running around) and characters (McNulty is as much a spoiler in law enforcement as Omar is in the drug trade) to maintain coherent plot lines. The show's style trains us to pay attention to everything, because anything might turn out to be mortally consequential, or not. Consider a scene in season three: in a gay bar, the camera catches an apparently accidental glimpse of Major Rawls, the toughest-talking cop in the show, who irrationally loathes the hopelessly hetero McNulty who in a pinch would fuck a stoat. But that's it. The camera ignores Rawls. We barely see him, don't really know why he's there, and the plot offers no follow-through; it's just something that happens.

The Wire doesn't just train *us* to pay attention: it dramatizes forms of attention. McNulty's is feral, like that of the rat-catching terrier in Omar's storyline: attention as animal pursuit. Avon's ("I'm just a gangsta, I suppose") fixes on force and control. String scrutinizes the business of drugs; when his attention gets divided by his ambitions as a real estate developer, it brings him to a crummy, smashingly staged end. Omar's deceptively sleepy attention *fastens* to things, whether it's taking down a dealer or helping a cop solve a crossword by providing "Ares" in place of "Mars." ("Same dude, different name, is all.") My personal favorite is Lester, builder of "toy furniture" and physically fearless cop who is also that rarest thing on TV, an adult who expresses believable methodical intellectualism. Sitting before the computer screens that cherry-pick info off the wire, he shows the same Cistercian attention as when he's making his "miniatures." And like nearly every major character, at some point Lester eventually narrates his own backstory, as do Kima, McNulty, Sibotka, Cutty, Bubbs, and others whose self-representations reveal character as it determines fate. Most recognize at least one fateful trait in others: decency, or at any rate an honesty that within the rules of the Game passes for decency. It's why Avon lets Cutty out of the Game, why D'Angelo knows Wallace is doomed, why Lester recognizes in a mere photograph the good nature of a bar girl in Avon's club, who subsequently becomes an informant. "She has that look," he says. "You know, she's a *citizen*." One especially sick-making passage comes in the fifth season when Lester lets his incorruptible attention be corrupted for political reasons: to bump police budgets, he helps falsify a story about serial murders.

The storylines are soaked with sardonic bitterness about the brokenness and unfixability of our institutions, and they make no apologies for despair. The only institution that works is what the street dealers call Hamsterdam, the junkie village created by the visionary police captain Bunny Colvin, who segregates all Baltimore drug trade to a few city blocks—a ghetto inside a ghetto—in order to liberate decent people and neighborhoods held hostage to drug culture. Its sanity is perceived and treated by authorities as craziness. David Simon, who created and watch-dogged *The Wire*, never tired of saying that it's about how capitalism cripples institutions. (The narcotics business rots coherent cultures.) The show demonstrates how Bunny's individual will, or the collective will of the detail that works the major drug cases, will either fail because it can't change the political culture it has to function in or will corrupt itself by imitating, with the best intentions, the cynical methods of the structures it tries otherwise to undermine. The trumped-up serial murders demonstrate how good police think they can swallow the devil's spit and still have the breath of angels. Characters in *The Wire* lead ambiguous lives. What makes it morally intense is that it dramatizes what it feels like to live not just *with* ambiguity but *for* it.

Fiction-making media (not just movies and TV but, as season five makes clear, newspapers too) fumble into drippy sentimentalism or stiffen into overly righteous emotion when dealing with grief. *The Wire* contains moments of grief uncompromised by special pleading or "framing," though the purity of feeling can't be separated from ambiguity. Nothing matches the elegiac grandeur of the spiritual, "Jesus On the Mainline," sung, *field-shouted,* at D'Angelo's funeral. Never mind it's mourning for and by a drug-running society. The song doesn't ask us to sympathize, only to witness grieving. And much later, the mere sight of the abandoned boarded-up houses where the newest drug lord Marlo has stashed bodies is an image of loss, of houses not as beds of culture but dumpsters for dead human beings: the houses represent all the species of concealment, misdirection, and devaluation of the human that every social order in *The Wire* is soaked in.

A word about "Hamsterdam." A word, I mean, about *The Wire*'s words. The dialogue doesn't sound squared-up or "written." It's just talk. The language of the Avon-Stringer-Marlo crews is a virus that spreads, as the series progresses, through other social orders. Their speech and the cops' can hardly be told apart. As the rough-around-the-edges politico Carcetti rises from City Councilman to Mayor, his speech crawls closer to the street. I still struggle to understand what the androgynous, homicidal enforcer Snoop is saying exactly, but I get the drift because of her slurred timing—her speech is like a rhythm section to the other voices around her. If the language of *The Wire* had bled into common usage (like Seinfeld's "yada-yada" and "soup Nazi") you'd have college political science professors answering student questions with "Because that's how they do" or "Ain't no thing." The feist-iest language match-up is between cops and crooks (drug crooks, I mean). They communicate by chopping language into bits, then leaving most of the bits out. The dealers don't fill in the blanks: they use ellipses as musical notation, they communicate by what they don't say, which is what makes getting good wire intelligence on them so maddening. The cops have their own cues and codes. In one scene, and an actor's dream, Bunk and McNutty, working with virtually no evidence, perfectly block out how a murder happened, their recognitions inflected exclusively with "fuck" and its offspring—"Fucketyfuck," "Uhn, fuck me . . . ," "Mother fuck!" etc.

The Wire works all the resources of the medium. Its music soundtrack is always ambient, usually blasting or crooning from cars, and never tells us how we're supposed to be feeling, though sometimes it tingles with humor, like the Temps' *Just My Imagi-nation* woo-ing from a car radio while Omar reconnoiters Marlo's digs. The visual rhythms are jumpy and impatient, but not manic in the way of a Paul Greengrass or a Tony Scott. The shoot-outs, except for personal, focused paybacks, are chaotic, on the run—we're as disoriented as the participants. The projects at night are lit to look like a cave culture that happens to possess an orange sofa. We flop from it and the lurid shooting galleries Bubbs frequents to the official lighting of City Hall and police headquarters. The camera, like all the moving parts of the various plots, won't stay put: the narrative eye prowls, glides, overrides.

The collective responsible for writing *The Wire* has its mind on children and the life span of innocence. Most viewers, I think, prefer season four, about a bunch of eighth-grade boys, because it's about foundational fatedness, character formation, nature-and-nurture. We watch moral consciousness becoming occluded or clarified by circumstance. One troublemaker named Namond is delivered from the drug life not just because of a policeman's inter-vention, but because he brings to their encounter some mystery of nature. All sorts of children are already lost souls or at risk. From the beginning of the series, McNulty's two sons are casualties of their father's obsessiveness. Carcetti's children are hostage to his political career. The cop Kima all but abandons the child she shares with her former girlfriend. In the opening scene I mentioned earlier, we see a community of children already being shaped by the models around them. *The Wire* argues darkly (but correctly) that the capitalist institutions we entrust the lives of children to (law enforcement, the courts, local government) will barter that trust in a second to self-interest and expediency. Corruption isn't just a familiar political virus, it's a society's soul rotting. Children also endure the lurking despair of an unreachable world elsewhere, best dramatized in one of my favorite exchanges, between the reformed ex-con Cutty and a pouty kid who works out at Cutty's fight gym. The kid, Dukie, is a terrible boxer because he lacks heart. He can't fight, he doesn't want to sell drugs, he really just wants to know one thing: "Like, how do you get from here to the rest of the world?" Cutty, who knows he can be only one kind of mentor, has to answer, "I wish I knew."

For street kids, life is an early onset firing process, hardening the soft metals of childhood into much harder alloys. We watch the forging take place at different ages, from the very young boy who shoots Omar to the young adult D'Angelo, a killer with a genuine sense of mercy who begins to question fatedness in ways that guarantee his death at the hands of the people who mentored him. The montage that ends the series includes: Dukie shooting up under the tutelage of the horse-cart trashpicker he works for, in a hovel they share with the horse, whose head leans over Dukie's shoulder like a mockery of the Nativity donkey; the very young boy who kills Omar being led away in cuffs; more kids of all ages sitting on stoops, dealing on corners, idling (loudly) in the projects. *The Wire* is so layered and rigged with resonances that after a couple of viewings, when I saw Omar get shot, I thought first that, like Ares, he's the Warrior-God of the projects, and second that he attributes his knowledge of the "same dude, different name" to having studied mythology at school ("I used to love them myths. That stuff was deep. Truly."). You can push this farther—the screenwriters let us—and know that Omar also would have learned that Ares was Aphrodite's brother, and that it's Omar who shows himself to be the most devoted, tender, sensual and, when his boyfriend Brandon is killed and mutilated, most murderously vindictive lover in the series. By the show's end, the apparently sweet-tempered and charitable Michael has taken Omar's place, robbing dealers, learning how to seem invincible and fearless, armed like Omar, as if in adulation, with a double-barreled.

A wire taps privacies; it transmits information that's clear or opaque; it bears whole sentences or fragments; it can close a circuit that connects numerous points of contact; it's a straight line that's really a web. If a wire lets cops follow the drugs, everything stays under control of official entities. But, as Lester says, if it lets them follow the *money*, nobody's in control. The wire will lead you into complex corruptions at every level of society. *The Wire* has its own tenacity of consciousness. It won't let go of things, and every bit at least *seems* wired to some other bit. Sometimes it carries and connects coherent stories, sometimes not. It's a dark essay on illusion and delusion. It tells us as often as we can stand to hear it that there are no simple answers, that much of the time we don't really know to ask the right questions. It dramatizes how we reveal our natures. A melancholy procession of images—city neighborhoods, industrial sites, people at work, street action, weathers—ends the series as it began, in instability, disorientation, uncertainty, and irresoluteness. It welcomes us again to the world of adults and adult-making.

2011

To Each His Own

There's no American novelist whose voice has the broad public resonance that Leonardo Sciascia's had. When an Italian critic sadly said to me, two years after Sciascia's death in 1989, that he was much missed, it wasn't a sentimental judgment. Sciascia was more than just a distinguished writer. He and his work were a critical, moral presence in Italian cultural life. He wrote regularly for the press and participated in the major polemics of the postwar period. He used storytelling as an instrument for investigating and attacking the ethos of a culture, the insular, mafia-saturated culture of Sicily, which he believed to be a metaphor of the world. The major novels, *A ciascuno il suo* (*To Each His Own,* or *A Man's Blessing*), *Il giorno della civetta* (*The Day of the Screech Owl*), *Il Consiglio d'Egitto* (*The Council of Egypt*), and *Il contesto* (*The Context*) are about political morality, though they are not political in content or moralizing in intent. Each is a genre piece, a detective story, but of an odd kind: when all clues are gathered and aligned, they lead to a wrong solution; or the mystery is insoluble because practically everyone involved, except the investigator, is duplicitous.

Born in 1921, one year before Mussolini's march on Rome, in the small Sicilian town of Recalmuto in the southwestern interior near Agrigento, Sciascia was brought up in a landscape of extremes—torrid summers and icy winters, sulfur mines and vineyards, quarries and wild fruit trees. In interviews with Marcelle

Padovani during the late 1970s, he commented on how strange it was to have grown up during the years of Fascism, to lead a double life as a child who hated Mussolini yet wore the obligatory school uniform: black shirt, tie pin embossed with the image of Il Duce, and tasseled black fez. He spent his first twenty years in what he called a "non-society society," a Pirandello-esque fiction made up of alienated, invisible, falsified or inauthentic creatures, a society grounded in deception and bad faith, "doubly unjust, doubly un-free, doubly irrational." Born to a culture of unreason, he became a French Enlightenment writer, although even before he discovered his literary heroes—Voltaire, Stendhal, Diderot ("He is my master")—Sciascia committed himself to reason as a fixed pivot. His commitment was so obsessive that in time it became what he called a "neurosis of reason," a rationality that skirted the edge of unreason.

The major novels are inquiries into the impossibility of justice and the terminal intellectual fatigue caused by disillusionment. Sciascia himself believed in the possibility of a free and just world, however imperfect, but the salient instrument in his fiction is skepticism. Skepticism as a means of social survival is also a core mafia value, so the skepticism cultivated by Sciascia was a moral inoculation against the mafia ethos. But it could also express itself as unintentional complicity. His gristly nonconformity reached its most compromised state when in 1987 this lifelong enemy of the mafia criticized members of the anti-mafia commission, who had cut more deeply into the mafia hierarchy than anyone since Mussolini, for being political opportunists. The accusation had unhappy consequences for Sciascia's image as a righteous public intellectual. It also showed what happens when skepticism outpaces or occludes facts. Whatever its dangers, Sciascia couldn't live without it. The "detective" in *A ciascuno il suo*, Professor Laurana, has a different problem. He fatally lacks the elastic, insistent, homeopathic skepticism that is rubbed so deeply and invisibly into the textures of Sciascia's narrative. Worse yet, he allows eros to foul the clarity of his investigation. He's more a feckless snoop than detective.

Society held hostage to a suffocating ethos of secrecy, silence, and misdirection; criminality as an expression of maniacal self-containment; evil as an all-powerful but apparently author-less entity (the mafia, Fascism, the Red Brigades); the monstrous perversions of loyalty, love, and honor sponsored by the mentality that is *mafia*—these are the real subjects of Sciascia's best novels. The epigraph to the Italian edition of *A ciascuno il suo*, which didn't appear in the 1968 English translation, comes from Poe's *The Murders in the Rue Morgue*: "Let it not be supposed that I am detailing any mystery or penning any romance." Sciascia later said that his intention had been to write a book about the political disillusionment and social chaos triggered by the failure of the 1964 coalition of Socialists and Christian Democrats, which had inspired hope for a balanced, stable, reasonably honest government. The failure of the coalition was partly responsible for the breakdown of public order that led to the violence of the 1970s, "*gli anni di piombo,*" the years of lead, which culminated in the 1978 kidnapping and execution of the Christian Democratic leader Aldo Moro by the Red Brigades. Even without the benefit of hindsight, when he wrote *To Each His Own* Sciascia knew that much was at stake and was disconcerted when the book was treated as a mafia story.

It *is* a mafia story, though it has little to do with the organization called the mafia, which Sciascia in the introduction to *Il giorno della civetta* defined as "a parasitic middle-class that exploits instead of producing," because it's about mafia as a systemic, irreducible set of assumptions and behaviors, often murderous, embedded in deceit and concealment. Well into the story, before we know who committed the two murders that begin the action, we learn that the lawyer Rosello, one of several cronies who gather daily in the piazza to trade gossip and philosophize on the state of things, has major business interests and is tied up in what people assume to be marginally but negligibly criminal enterprises. But he's most admired for his political canniness. As a provincial Counselor, Rosello manages to swing his recalcitrant Christian Democratic Council into an alliance with the Socialists. This ambiguous, dangerous man engineers the so-called "historic compromise" Sciascia had in mind when he wrote the book.

"I don't have a great creative imagination," Sciascia said in the Padovani interviews. "All my books are the story of a series of historical delusions seen in the light of the present." Rosello, architect of hope in postwar Italian politics, also designs the double murders that begin the story. The town pharmacist, having just received a poison pen death threat that he takes as a joke, goes hunting with a respected local physician, Dr. Roscio, and both are killed for no apparent reason. The town is immediately infested by a plague of hypotheses and attributions. Sciascia dramatizes from the inside out how a community will fabricate the appearance of truth from a tissue of unsubstantiated insinuations, usually because it needs to believe the worst of human beings, though as it turns out this is far from the worst. The murders are assumed to be a classic instance of a cuckold avenging the pharmacist's presumed affair with a girlfriend. Dr. Roscio, unlucky soul, was killed because he was a witness.

Professor Laurana, a diffident and quiet-spoken schoolteacher, is drawn into the mystery when he notices that a piece of the threatening letter was clipped from the Vatican newspaper, the *Osservatore Romano*, which he recognizes from its masthead: "*Unicuique suum.*" To each his own. The newspaper is a clue to the crime. The motto, though he'll realize it only when it's too late, is a clue to Laurana's fate. He's certainly an unlikely detective hero. He's a timid, sexually repressed Mama's boy; the narrator describes him as "an honest, meticulous, melancholy man; not very intelligent and indeed at times positively obtuse." He's astute and Sicilian enough, however, to know that appearances shouldn't be trusted, that niceties often mask wickedness. After an amiable interview with the rector, a likable man, Laurana reminds himself that "Sicily is full of likable people who should have their heads chopped off." But his belief in the supremacy of reason and candor over irrationality and silence can't save him from a pathology that infects his culture: the silent complicity that allows those who know who committed the killings and why—nearly *everyone* around him knows—to withhold their knowledge from him. In this culture, self-possessiveness is a shield against the incipient evil intentions of others. By covering over the erotic and political connections that implicate Rosello and Roscio's widow, the townspeople can possess secret knowledge without exercising the power such knowledge confers. In the presence of evil, their culture not only allows but insists on silent reserve and privileged gossip over confrontation and exposure.

Sciascia's plain diction gives his work a cool, canny tone, but his complex, bristly syntax enacts the connivances and uncertainties that drive the plot. It's an acidic style that criticizes while it discloses, that can mimic the sophistry, the rotted grandiloquence, which is the dominant idiom of the culture. In his angular, mock-innocent observations of social behavior, he out-Stendhals Stendhal. Immediately after the killings most of the town gossip is about the hunting dogs who "report" the killings by returning without their masters. "The return of the dogs set the whole town to disputing for days and days (as will always happen when people discuss the nature of dogs) about the order of Creation, since it is not at all fair that dogs should lack the gift of speech."

Like all of Sciascia's novels, *A ciascuno il suo* is filled with exquisitely oblique, disputatious conversations. In an interview Laurana conducts with Dr. Roscio's aged father, the old rationalist makes a distinction between Sicily and "the North." A northerner who hears the proverb, "The dead are dead; help the living," imagines an accident that leaves one man dead and another injured, so you let the dead man be and help the survivor. A Sicilian hearing the same proverb imagines instead a murderer and his victim, and if the victim is your own flesh and blood you help the living man by expediting his way to hell. In this elegantly brutal book, even that code is turned on its head. It's Professor Laurana who is sent packing to hell—he ends up buried in a *sulfur* mine—not a victim of someone's vengeance, merely a scraped-off residue which would have gummed up the political-erotic watchworks designed by Rosello and the widow Roscio, while the townspeople stand by in complicit, self-protective, rigorous silence.

Sciascia is the rare novelist who has been well served by movie makers, in part because the directors who turned his work into film—Elio Petri (*A ciascuno il suo*), Damiano Damiani (*Il giorno della civetta*), and Francesco Rosi (*Il contesto*, released as *Cadaveri eccellenti*)—had similar leftist leanings and critical social awareness. But there's another reason. In his childhood and adolescence Sciascia was not only a reader of prodigious, Coleridgean appetites, he was also a great movie fan, especially of the silents, and he once admitted that his way of writing owed more to the cinema than to literature. Although the final line of Petri's very good 1969 movie adaptation, released here under the silly title *We Still Kill the Old Way,* doesn't appear in the novel, it's true to Sciascia's merciless and icily comic vision of evil. The line is spoken by a cynically admiring townsman at the wedding of Rosello and Roscio's widow who, it turns out, are cousins raised in the same house and in love since childhood: "*Hanno fatto un vero capolavoro.*" They pulled off a real masterpiece.

2000

On Not Reading Fiction

A friend who reads mostly fiction, and who knows I mostly don't, was surprised when I gave her a birthday gift of the Sicilian writer Leonardo Sciascia's *Il Contesto*. We'd been talking about Matteo Garrone's recent movie, *Gomorrah*, about the Camorra, Naples' equivalent of the mafia. (Southern regions have different names for it: in Calabria it's called *'Ndrangheta*.) Sciascia wrote many books and is one of those writers enormously honored and read in his own country but who, even with the heroic efforts of the New York Review Classics series to bring back and keep in print a handful of titles, remains pretty much a blank here. Most of Sciascia's fiction has to do nominally not with the mafia exactly, but with *"mafia*," the viral, evidently incurable social-political-criminal organism that for a long time has determined the functioning (or malfunctioning) of the body politic in Sicily and other regions.

Il Contesto (published under the title *Equal Danger*) translates literally as *The Context* but trails associated meanings: "setting," "web," "netting," "matrix." It follows a police investigator named Rogas as he tries to solve the mystery of serial murders of judges in an unnamed but presumably Latin American city. He's an Enlightenment realist trying to execute his duties in an otherwise poisoned, conniving judicial crony system. Rogas does what detectives do. He amasses information, he sees that all the murders are clearly connected, and when he's finally about to crack his case, the case is cracked over his poor head. When he meets with a journalist who promises to help him solve the murders, both are murdered. No suspects. End of investigation. Nobody solves anything, but something does triumph. Not justice or conscience but the "context."

While reading it, my friend Beth sends an email raving about the book, then next day I get a distress signal: The serial murders aren't solved! And who kills Rogas and the journalist? Doesn't Sciascia owe his readers some hint of who the culprit is? In my overlong, contorted reply, I struggled to answer (and calm) her, until I finally identified the dissonance between her dismay and my enthusiasm, not only regarding *Il Contesto* but also Sciascia's other major things: *To Each His Own, The Day of the Owl, The Council of Egypt.* I take pleasure from them because it's not the content of narrative that engages me, it's narrative style. Who cares about plot? Or character development? When I want character development and heavy plotting, I read Dickens and Hardy or watch *The Wire*.

The *Contesto* situation was obvious: Beth reads fiction for different reasons than I do, which maybe explains why she reads so much of it. Sciascia in Italian is a sly, never flashy, queasily insinuating stylist, and because he writes in the plain style, the canniness and insinuation can be very adequately brought over into English. The way his sentences coil around an idea and enact the disorienting range of possible explanations for any event along with the mutual nose-biting of reason and unreason in the political sphere, the way the sentences, in other words, do their dance of ideation and connivance—this gives me satisfying formal delight. Sciascia doesn't just lay out the facts of a case that finally harmonize to form a whole, digestible truth. He uses syntax to graph the wobbly operations of hazard and uncertainty.

The flurries of novels and story collections puffed and huzzah-ed every week in (pick your style of wallpaper) *The New York Times Book Review, The London Review of Books,* and *The New York Review of Books* flash past this reader like tiny iridescent fish schooling behind aquarium glass. They look so pretty, and see how they swoop and prowl. I don't have any reasonable (or, for that matter, unreasonable) bias against most fiction. It just bores me. Plot, paid out in a one-step-in-front-of-the-other manner or a by-the-numbers arc or cleverly fragmented and shuffled into different time zones and voices, bores me. But a novel made of sentences that are less interested in organizing information or shaping action than they are in graphing a shape of feeling about the very material being matrixed, composed of prose rhythms that can be now lugubrious, now mercurial, swift or chuggy, dodgy or nastily assertive, all in service of making a shape of mindful feeling—*that* I can read. I'm not saying I'm right, I'm only saying this is how it is. Of Don De Lillo's novels, I can enter *Falling Man, Libra,* or *Underworld* virtually at random: even if I'm not quite oriented to what's going on, it doesn't matter because what's going on is a passion of discovery. Breaking into Cormac McCarthy's *Blood Meridian* at any chapter is like breaking into any major scene in *Lear.* I don't feel as if I'm following the sentences of O'Connor's "A Good Man Is Hard to Find," "Good Country People," and "The Life You Save May Be Your Own," I feel as if I'm riding them. Every time I read these, the phrase-by-phrase dynamics (cadences, tonalities, speeds) change. Whatever the gifts of Phillip Roth, Toni Morrison, Joyce Carol Oates, or Ian McEwan, or for that matter Ross MacDonald and Thomas Perry, and I've read my share of them all, they don't write sentences that excite and draw me in, though they're fine for what they are: the equivalent of middlebrow TV.

Even a book in translation can have its stylish charms, as we know from the Pevear and Volokhonsky translations of Dostoyevsky (their *Demons* most of all), whom they've released from the contrived elegance laid on by other translators and revealed the deliberately uneven, antiqued, broken-up style that for years Russian scholars protested was missing from available translations. But let me stay in the time frame. The week after the Sciascia brush fire between me and Beth, a poet friend who also reads very little fiction suggested I try *Metropole*, by Ferenc Karinthy, that renowned Hungarian writer-of-all-trades and water polo champion. So, wise guy of any type, how judge for its style a novel written in Hungarian? Because the translator, Georges Szirtes, a tough-minded Anglo-Hungarian poet, has performed, my instincts tell me, a more than adequate equivalent of sentences and paragraphs, a mentality really, that imitates the vertiginous, hermetic, madcap, dire dynamics of the original.

Metropole's context: A Hungarian linguist named Budai, on his way to a conference in Helsinki, somehow ends up on the wrong flight and arrives at an unidentifiable destination, unidentifiable because he has entered a parallel world, "off" but normalized in its own queerness, a reality that makes Alice look like a piker. Deposited in a civilization where he doesn't even vaguely recognize the language, though he's on fair terms with nearly two dozen languages from all the major language groups, Budai is immediately rendered illiterate: he can neither communicate with or understand what's said by the citizens of this mysterious place, who themselves, to his trained but baffled ear, seem to speak different languages or dialects, though not all the time. At one point Budai thinks "that each of the city's inhabitants might be speaking his own language, that there were as many languages as there were people." Just as he recognizes the language at least as being a language, though one he can't penetrate, he recognizes the place itself as a busy city, but it's a busyness catastrophically amped and revved: wherever he goes, to hotel, Metro, street, shops, church, there are exasperating queues, dense manic mobs of citizens rushing everywhere, and out-of-sight bumper-to-bumper traffic nuttily speeding or at a standstill (neither for any apparent reason). Like one of Sciascia's investigators, Budai, an analytical, self-possessed mid-twentieth-century man of reason, finds himself in a society he recognizes as a society—its architectural and behavioral structures are immediately familiar to us—but doesn't really comprehend. Unlike a Sciascia protagonist, he's stuck in a context where he can't even cipher the language:

beneficiary of a cruel beneficence, he therefore can't be deceived or misled. Drowning in torrents of context rushing toward him, this erudite man shrinks to idiocy.

Metropole has no plot to speak of, only events, no one of which seems to proceed by any narrative logic to another: there are only disconnected *instances* of life. There's little characterization, because that depends on speech, the production or understanding of it, or the inferring of the meanings of gestures that itself is grounded in language. (Different cultures have different gestures for "no.") Instead of characters there are indifferent, spiritless types, because language is one gateway to the soul, even if it's a corrupt soul practicing a delusive or falsifying language. But all this, for me—and I'm only talking about taste or predilection, an idiolect as much as the *bibby-turpii-uurdii-bibibi* speech of the book's population—is a colorful lure guaranteed to send me right down the rabbit hole, yipping and laughing all the way. And the reason hasn't to do with verbal style, obviously, at least not entirely, since the book was written in Hungarian, but my taste test for translation is if the English text sounds like something a crafty human being might actually have written. (See Joachim Neugroschel's and Mark Harman's bluff, deadpan-comic retranslations of Kafka.) Like good poetry, *Metropole* operates by a skill set of inherited conventions (manipulating persons, places, times, events) that are set in motion by an internal logic that causes every unit of composition (sentence or verse line) in some way to reverb or weave through another. Which is a way of saying that, just as a poem is a momentary revelation of the razor wire coils of consciousness in the stream of time, this novel, like Sciascia's work, possesses an idiosyncratic coherent mind of its own. If there's a story, it's nested in the surprising serial disclosures of that consciousness.

The style that matters is a style of fanatical mind that constellates bits of language into fresh patterns. (Other scriptural texts: "The Dead" and *Portrait of the Artist as a Young Man; Speak, Memory* and *Lolita*). The matter of style is a moveable feast. Too much poetry of our moment is bland, studied, inconsequential. Or it deals in jerry-rigged revelation. I prefer work that in its laying out of words surprises itself as it goes along, instant by instant. Like the moment when Budai and a hotel elevator operator, whom he (mistakenly) thinks he's managed to communicate with, steal a kiss while she's on her smoke break: they both *come upon* that intimate moment as a space in time delivered from the crushing, bullying imperatives and preliminaries and structures that freight successful communication. Any American vagabond can have a hot time with a Basque girl who speaks no English because they can communicate with the body's language of sexuality and appreciate that such communication is useful and good. But neither the girl or Budai knows how to begin to interpret what leads to the kiss or what it means. Then, in one of the few moments of shared understanding (which is to say, shared bafflement) with the reader, they part as if nothing happened. The mind of the novel, its style, validates the moment and its hallowed meaning, because style, which legislates itself, legislates also how the mind apprehends a perfectly strange, invented, irrational order.

2009

Voices in My Room

Fat

(War Poets)

A plain at dawn. Clear air. The sun rising quicker than it should. Dust stirs on the horizon. The more visible and abrasive it is, the more ghastly, smothering itself like surf. Clamor growls inside the dust, louder by the moment, now different textures grinding together in the mix. Wheels, car horns, shouts, engines of some kind, stomping, reedy Asian-sounding music, tank treads, then shapes that swim into articulated forms, soldiers of some kind, chariots, armor, archers and armored vehicles, coming for death or glory or both. I pray God be with me, to protect me and sponsor my killing. I start downhill and feel a multitude pounding around me knee high in the dust. We've become what they've become, a death-seeking dirt storm. We're all sick with dread and fever and exhilaration.

Over the years that scene, or film clip, has become a primal site in my imagination. It's a composite of recurrent nightmares, Sam Peckinpah's *The Wild Bunch*, boyhood adventure-book daydreaming, Cormac McCarthy's *Blood Meridian*, and street confrontations between gangs when I was a kid. The *Iliad* is part of the compound. But my dream scene isn't Homeric, it's mere sensibility, subjective, without an ethic or culture to give reason to its menace. The only Homeric thing missing is everything: courage, honor, ceremony, prowess, convention, loyalty, gods. And yet its feeling tone is sat-

urated by something Simone Weil finds in these lines from Book
22 of the *Iliad*:

> *And Andromache ordered her bright-haired maids in the palace*
> *To place on the fire a large tripod, preparing*
> *A hot bath for Hector, returning from battle.*
> *Foolish woman! Already he lay, far from hot baths,*
> *Slain by grey-eyed Athena, who guided Achilles' arm.*

While Andromache prepares Hector's welcome, Achilles is dragging her Prince behind his chariot, dead and stripped of his armor.
Weil: "Far from hot baths he was indeed, poor man. And not he
alone. Nearly all the *Iliad* takes place far from hot baths. Nearly
all of human life, then and now, takes place far from hot baths."
Because she was writing in 1940, her essay on the poem was tough-
ened by recent events. Her *Iliad* is "a poem of force" because force
turns whatever it affects into a thing. "Exercised to the limit, it
turns man into a thing in the most literal sense: it makes a corpse
out of him." Or something not even quite a corpse but a lumpy,
oleaginous mass. The firestorms whipped up by the 1943 Allied
bombing of Hamburg—heavy bombs blew out doors and walls,
incendiaries ignited rooftops and upper stories, then medium-sized
bombs blasted lower stories—left behind mounds of bodies whose
fat had melted in the heat and congealed.

◉◉◉

Poetry's affects are practically infinite, from unconditional joy to
unredeemable anguish, with manifold minutely calibrated feel-
ing-states in between. I've especially come to value (though not to
the exclusion of all else) a fairly narrow range: uncertainty, anxiety,
irresoluteness, ambiguity, bleared comedy. And with these a variety
of emotional engines: disruptiveness, disconcerting surprise, desta-
bilization, and mixed tones. I know that one of poetry's traditional

powers is to console and heal. Shaman-talk, liturgies, poems that extend condolence or sympathy or wishes for good fortune. The strongest of this kind absorbs into song tragic knowledge—that we are of nature and will die—such that the hope of healing is veined with the dark matter of our own death. What matters just as much as its power to heal is poetry's power to open lesions in consciousness, to upset our most precious balances, to give away (without crowing over) the darker tints in our nature, what's most delusional, nebulous, avaricious, covetous, or painfully relativist. If the work is good, it will enfold the pleasures of formal energies, design, and recognition, whatever the subject, and be a carnival of intensest spirit, of vexed fields of relatedness between us and ourselves, the individual and the common, the human and its nature.

I return to certain modern poems because they bestride ambiguous boundaries. In Hardy's "At a Watering Place," two men sitting on an esplanade watch a happy, betrothed couple walk past. One confides to the other that he knows what the intended groom does not: "That dozens of days and nights on end / I have stroked her neck, unhooked the links / Of her sleeve to get at her upper arm . . ." He confides in his chum what he's certain the bride-to-be will never confide to her future husband. He shares knowledge with her but not his power to disclose. He seals the tacit pact and casually hurrahs the groom's humiliation by pasting over it a trivializing cliché: "Well, bliss is in ignorance: what's the harm!" That last line leaves me queasy. There's *always* harm, and the poem is the shape of it.

◉◉◉

The *Iliad* dramatizes the awful absoluteness and bloodiness of warrior culture, a celebration of killing prowess so complete that it can leave us feeling chagrined and a little sick at heart for having thrilled to slaughter. But its greatness lies in the episodes of compassion, wisdom, deliberation, domestic solicitude and sorrow, and the daily round of habit and custom interleaved with the events that the presence of Helen brings about. Achilles' rage is the song's subject, but Homer writes into battlefield chaos the life of nature outside that field, of orders of culture that share the earth with warrior princes but whose tones and textures are worlds apart. In the first major battle scenes late in Book 4, the Trojan archer Pandarus shoots a fatal arrow at Menelaus who at the last second is shielded by Athena, who "skewed the tearing shaft, / flicking it off your skin as quick as a mother / flicks a fly from her baby sleeping softly." (Fagles) The figure fuses the man-killing society of warriors and immortals who protect them to the settled households of mothers and babes, disparate but contiguous worlds bonded by different sorts of loyalty.

Homer's material world consists of relatively few parts, but he integrates its necessary parts so exactly that we feel we know *all* the particulars of that world. Most of the particulars have to do with war. The fighting on the fields of Troy is a chaos composed of formulaic, almost mechanized movements that tabulate and ceremonialize the efficiency of slaughter. Its economy of horror is precise. Homeric grammar has a dual number for things in twos. When a spear is thrust between a warrior's eyes, the anatomical exactitude gives the action a hard, precise beauty that in modern readers can induce a dread inseparable from thrills. Cormac McCarthy's *Blood Meridian*, a cowboy book about the maraudings of scalp hunters in Mexico, creates a similar confounding and tests the moral boundaries of empathetic excitements. But in McCarthy's novel human beings, especially the demiurge character called The Judge, are evil agents, not killer heroes but death dispensers. The evil entity in the *Iliad* is death, which comes swiftly and a thousand times over and ends all we know of the brief, bright world of the senses.

◎◎◎

The pieties of war are an oraborus. They're like the pieties surrounding the right to bear arms: the patriot Charleton Heston and anarchist militiamen meet, rifles raised, shouting, "From my cold dead hands!" Likewise, absolute pacificism and absolute jingoism each believe that God or Absolute Principle is on its side, which has the irreducible moral value of being right. Neither side can hear the other's reasons, even if they could stand to listen. Many of us tell ourselves that if the race is to survive, and we have science along with instincts to help us in the task, we have to do what we're incapable of doing—doing without war. That knowledge, and the amassed facts of human waste and loss that go with it, could make for good, maybe great, poetry. But it would be poetry hot with ambiguity and the conflictedness of knowing that even when we propose answers, we know there are none, because there is no certitude. I can conceive of poetry that responds to the politically tribalized bloodshed of our planet's small, constant wars with a correspondingly blunt complexity, a poem that ignores neither the horror nor the thrill of killing. A Vietnam vet who became a history professor once told me how he loved being last man to leave a village because last man out torched it.

◉◉◉

The *Iliad* weaves its world out of likeness. The whiteness of Achaeans covered with kicked-up dust and soon to be harvested by death is like the heaps of white chaff on a farm's threshing floor at harvest time. Homer likens the dark amassed battalions readied for action behind Big and Little Ajax to the gathering black storm that frightens a goatherd into driving his flock into coves. The poem documents again and again the terror and contingency of existence. Sarpedon, Patroclus, Diomedes, Achilles, Menelaus, and the other great fighters all thrive in that medium. In *Iliad* 5 Diomedes is killing anybody who comes at him. He goes after and grievously wounds Ares, "a maniac, / born for disaster, double-dealing, / lying, two-faced god." Diomedes stabs him with a spear (he's already wounded Ares' sister, Aphrodite, and sent her weeping to her father in heaven) and when he extracts it "the brazen god of war let loose a shriek, roaring, / thundering loud as nine, ten thousand combat soldiers / shriek with Ares' fury when massive armies clash." Ares is unstoppably bellicose, a battlefield virus, pure compass-less mayhem. Like the other gods, he's not just a "figure" but a principle, a sponsoring agency. He's *the-state-of-being-murderous*. The British poet and screenwriter (and sometime movie actor) Christopher Logue was born to translate Ares into a contemporary idiom, although his latest versions out of Homer don't include the fight between Diomedes ("murderous Diomed, aka the Child") and Ares. No need. His enterprise transpires under the sign of the manic war god. Ares is the covering genius of the place, storming across every page.

◉◉◉

Background. In 1959 the classicist D. S. Carne-Ross was commissioning a new translation of the *Iliad* for BBC and suggested Logue contribute. Logue, who died in 2011, knew no Greek but availed himself of Carne-Ross's expertise and declared his strategy early on. Working from a trot, he would "concoct a storyline based on its main incident; and then, knowing the gist of what this or that character said, try to make their voices come alive and to keep the action on the move." He prepped by reading older translations, all the way back to Chapman's 1611 version. Thus he produced the Patrocleia, *Iliad* 16, in which Achilles' darling, the young Patroclus, wearing his friend's armor, fights Hector and is set up for the kill by Hector's protector, Apollo ("the Mousegod"). Logue went after essentials: force, scale, intimacy, metaphorical invention, and rakehell immediacy. Guided by Pope's remark that a translator of the Iliad "is above all things to keep alive that Spirit and Fire which makes his chief Character," and by Doctor Johnson's remark about the merit of any translation, that "We must try its effect as an English poem," Logue's intention was "to make a poem in

English dependent on the *Iliad*." In addition to the *Patrocleia*, he has produced *Kings* (Books 1 and 2), *Husbands* (3-4), *War Music* (16-19) and his newest, *All Day Permanent Red: The First Battle Scenes of the Iliad Rewritten.*

All Day Permanent Red (the name of a lipstick) is the punchiest and riskiest installment yet, beginning with its title and perfect cover image of a German policewoman crouched beside a meat wagon holding a pistol, her stocking feet lifted slightly out of her loafers. Perfect because it aligns with the anachronisms that jag through Logue's enterprise. A waist-to-shoulder wound is like a beauty queen's sash, the unpremeditated thrill of danger is "the Uzi shuddering warm against your hip," the Trojan Palt's chariot is "Porsche-fine" (Palt is an invented character, as are Gray, Chylab-borak, Quibuph, and the cribbed-from-Céline Bubblegum), the Greek army standing like the rising slats of a "raked sky-wide Venetian blind." These do more than "update" the events, they mediate brilliantly the force and visual particularizations of actions in Homer.

Logue cannily brings over very close equivalents of Homeric events. His description of Palt's death, "now on his hands and knees, / Holding the slick blue-greenish loops of his intestines up / Though some were dragging in the dust," answers to the fall of Diores in *Iliad* 4, whose "guts uncoiled, spilling loose on the ground." Homer, describing how "the savage work" of killing went on between Argives and Trojans—he uses the same word, *ergon*, for work and for what men do in battle—"mauling each other there like wolves, leaping, / hurtling into each other, man throttling man," is answered by Logue's "Half-naked men, brave, fit, loyal, fit, slab-sided men / Leaping onto each other like wolves / Screaming, kicking, slicing, hacking, ripping." Logue has a spe-cial genius for metaphors that cross-grain the narrative to shape meaning. I'm writing in 2003, during the Iraq War, a historical moment when we're so close to the direct connection between media-driven political manipulations and wartime deaths (all those journalist imbeds in the desert) that the figure of Diomed's shield sprouting "as many arrows on his posy shield / As microphones on politicians' stands" jumps alive with contemporary truth. His style has the popping all-at-onceness of *Briggflatts*, and the jigsaw pep of the *Cantos*; consequently, Logue's dynamics can get over-muscled, too push-pull, metrical energies switching in a heartbeat from draggy to propulsive. Film language is everywhere. The narrative enacts equivalents of master shots, close-ups, swish pans, montage, and rack focus. At one point, as Odysseus is about to say something to Idomeneo, Logue—who acted in Ken Russell's *The Devils* and relishes his own devilishness—pauses to say, "as we go tight."

The *Iliad* is great not only because of the extraordinary execution of its parts—the battles, the counsels, the naming of tribes and histories, the relations between mortal and immortal orders—but because it is, within the definitions of the culture, complete. The endless killing is overcast, via simile or scene change, by domestic or agrarian or shepherding imagery, like Hector's visit to his son and the "hot baths" he will never take, and above all by the ending of the poem, when Priam, led by Hermes through the Greek encampment, entreats Achilles to release Hector's body, which for days the Great Killer has been dragging around the tomb of Patroclus, though the Prince's body (thanks to his divine protectors) remains mysteriously intact . When Priam says, "I have endured what no one on earth has ever done before— / I put to my lips the hand of the man who killed my son," there's no Christian healing of enmity. What happens is that the Killer, the sort of hero who, as Erich Auerbach somewhere says, can only think Achillean thoughts, is restored to a completer sensation of human-ness, for Priam's words recall the death of his own father. In her fine little book about the poem, Rachel Bespaloff says that this is the only moment in the poem when supplication "sobers the man to whom it is addressed instead of exasperating him," a man for whom "cruelty is a sort of paroxysm of irritation in pursuit and counterstroke." When Achilles takes Priam's hand then gently pushes him away, both sharing memories of fathers and sons and death, the silence that momentarily comes between them, like quieted surf between roaring breakers, is the momentary suspension of all the worst noise of killing that is the poem's dominant music. Momentary because Achilles abruptly loses patience with the old man twice during the interview.

Bespaloff also says that the *Iliad* "antedates the divorce between nature and existence," a split grotesquely irremediable in James Dickey's "The Firebombing," a poem derived from 38 combat missions he flew as a radar observer in the Pacific Theater, which describes war *against*, not *out of* nature. On the field of Troy Ares is a tempestuous weather generated by the passions of men and gods. Aerial bombardment creates weathers, too, hellish screaming atmospheres—it's a technology of killing that usurps the prerogatives of the gods and any notion of fatedness. World War I had its poppies, which flourished in the churned-up lime of detonated terrain, flowering once the artillery shelling had passed, red with the blood of Englishmen. Poppies were grave markers. In World War II, aerial bombardment was death from above, a mockery of divine intervention and natural forces, meant to destroy a culture, not just win a battle, and its distinctly un-poppyish markers were melted bodies and chopped-down cityscapes.

◉◉◉

We sometimes speak of World War I poetry as if it were a communal voice (though no voices are more different that Wilfred Owen's and Isaac Rosenberg's), but I never even conceived a similar category—World War II poetry—until I read Harvey Shapiro's *Poets of World War II*. As a body of work, all by Americans, including Europeanized ones like Pound and H.D., it's more finely inflected in its lament, rage, delerium, argument, and recollection, than the work of the Great War poets. Nearly every poem is riven by some sort of conflictedness or ambiguity, even poems by a conscientious objector like William Stafford and a near-ideologue like Thomas McGrath. Another anthology, *Poets Against the War*, collects poems culled from the 13,000 emailed to its editor, Sam Hamill, in response to Laura Bush's cancellation of a White House poetry event when she learned she'd be presented with poems protesting the (then imminent) invasion of Iraq. Good intentions, viable positions, assertions of conscience, moral passion certainly all much on display. Poetry can absorb into its bloodstream all of that. But *they* aren't *it*. Hamill's anthology is a slab of adversarialism whacking against an adamant, arrogant, hermetic White House. I'm not here to rip into it. Its canned rectitude has been gleefully mocked by neocon media peddling its own canned product. But the poems, I have to say, aren't very good, mostly because they concede the resources of the medium, especially the formal dynamics that can make powerful, astute arguments. If you give these up, you're left with little more than sensibility. My opening fantasia was a display of mere sensibility, juried entirely by subjective experience, essential to lyric poetry but superfluous to politicized experience unless subjectivity has absorbed a vision of public life. (My favorite instance of this is Yeats's "Parnell's Funeral," where the quivering visionary implicates himself in the crude moralistic obtuseness that brought down a great leader.) The poets in Shapiro's anthology took for granted that if poetry's ancient resources are suspended in the name of something else, it becomes screed, petition, or propaganda. Nothing in *Poets Against the War*, which I'll return to later, comes close to the political comprehensiveness of Jarrell's famous "The Death of the Ball Turret Gunner," and the garish humor of annihilation that rises like bile in the last line:

> From my mother's sleep I fell into the State,
> And I hunched in its belly till my wet fur froze.
> Six miles from earth, loosed from its dream of life,
> I woke to black flak and the nightmare fighters.
> When I died they washed me out of the turret with a hose.

Jarrell didn't fight. He spent the war stateside, in the Army Air Forces, teaching—as a critic-poet might—celestial navigation. The hose down was described to him by a pilot. The poem is a bitter representation of the human as Weil's "things," and is of the same species of imagery as Hamburg's civilians turned to gobs of fat, but it could just as well turn up in an anthology about modern religiosity, because it's about beliefs, spurious or authentic, that sustain and maybe kill.

◉◉◉

World War II poets weren't constructing a moral-political record as Owen and Sassoon did, in part because the events they describe are truly apocalyptic—"Death from Above!"—and in part because their stories aren't meant to be corrective or edifying. We never feel we're being instructed. These are not (as many of Hamill's poets are) scolds. John Ciardi, best known now for his Dante translation but who once had some reputation as a poet, wrote his keenest work in response to wartime experience. He's best when nasty. His doggerel funereal music sounds like castanets carved of skull bones:

> *Here lie Ciardi's bones*
> *In their ripe organic mess.*
> *Jungle blown, his chromosomes*
> *Breed to a new address.*

When their island was being overrun, Japanese forces retreated to caves and coves where you can still find hardware, mess kits, and skeletons. Amputees and shell-shocked vets were emblems of World War I poetry. The spoor of World War II poems are jellied deposits. From Ciardi's "Elegy for a Cove Full of Bones:"

> *Death is lastly a debris*
> *Folding on the folding sea:*

Blanket, boxes, belts, and bones,
And a jelly on the stones.

At the other end of experiential exposure are poems by Allen Tate and Yvor Winters that implicate the muse. Tate's "Ode to Our Young Pro-Consuls of the Air" is about a poet who spends so much time in books that he overlooks catastrophe. ("What might I have done / (A poet alone?) / To balk or slay / These enemies of mind?") The nervous, contorted meditation strikes its weirdest note when Tate rhymes "Eliotic" with "patriotic." Winters, a poet always driven to find moral purpose and meaning beyond ongoing self-adjusting change, inquires into the purpose of the "blunt emblem" of the infantryman's rifle, and he gives voice to the non-Homeric body politic that Elias Canetti said is defined by that nineteenth-century-minted entity, the mass:

Impersonal the aim
Where giant movements tend;
Each man appears the same;
Friend vanishes from friend.

Syntax models feeling. Consider Edgar Bowers' "The Stoic: For Laura Von Courten," an elegy that memorialized bombed-out Munich, Venice ("sinking by degrees / Into the very water that she lights"), and Berlin, where a lion, set loose by an aimless strike on the city zoo, killed someone fleeing the raid. Bowers' last lines are all tiding moral deliberation enacted by syntax:

And by yourself there standing in the chill
You must, with so much known, have been afraid
And chosen such a mind of constant will,

Which, though all time corrode with constant hurt,
Remains, until it occupies no space,

That which it is; and passionless, inert,
Becomes at last no meaning and no place.

The Great War poets were outraged by lost illusions and prop-
agated their disillusionment. American World War II poets had
their own rhetoric of smithereened illusions, but it's more internalized. They weren't trying to convince anyone except themselves.
They lived with a sickening sense of derangement and randomness.
(Even Anthony Hecht's senatorial loftiness yielded to the extremities of his war experience.)They fought a war soggy with the
blood of new facts, even when, as in Jarrell's case, the facts weren't
experienced first hand. That didn't prevent Jarrell from exercising
the self-agonizing imagination and writing about the irresolvable
ambiguity of soldier-killers:

> *I have suffered, in a dream, because of him*
> *Many things; for this last savior, man,*
> *I have lied as I lie now. But what is lying?*
> *Men wash their hands, in blood, as best they can:*
> *I find no fault in this just man.*

The mournfulness in so many of these poems is a heavy mineral
element in the soul, unreachable, available only approximately in
words. Thomas McGrath, stationed in the Aleutians, wrote about
the nightmare of dead multitudes, himself among them:

> *I search for my comrades, and suddenly—there—there—*
> *Harry, Charlie, and Bob, but their faces are worn, old,*
> *And mine is among them. In a dream as real as war,*
> *I see the vast stinking Pacific suddenly awash*
> *Once more with bodies, landings on all beaches,*
> *The bodies of dead and living gone back to appointed places.*

There are many good and some great poems in Shapiro's anthology. H.D.'s subdued report of an encounter with an R.A.F. officer has her impeccable formal etiquette, silky with compassion but not precious. And George Oppen's bleached-bone manner creates poetry that's the verbal equivalent of negative space: we see not the chair but the space that defines it and, therefore, the chair itself. The passage from "Of Being Numerous" beginning "I cannot even now / Altogether disengage myself / From those men" is one of the great American poems about public and private domains. From the powerful awareness of solidarity with others in wartime he passes (in twenty flinty lines) to a vision of postwar America, of an eviscerated public life:

> *Within the walls*
> *Of cities*
>
> *Wherein their cars*
>
> *Echo like history*
> *Down walled avenues*
> *In which one cannot speak.*

The most overwhelming piece of poetry is James Dickey's "The Firebombing." Images, placid and ripping, of twenty years of routine, suburban, home-owning calm shuffle like phantasmagoria with cockpit views of a bombing raid on a Japanese landscape and the fuel-and-napalm cocktail the pilot spills onto civilians. Those gluey fires also coat the material well-being of postwar life:

> *golf carts and fingernail*
> *Scissors as yet unborn   tennis shoes*
> *Grocery baskets   toy fire engines*
> *New Buicks stalled by the half moon.*

The poem is itself a monstrous whirligig flying to pieces which, like Japanese cities, come to rest finally as "the apotheosis of gelatin."

◉◉◉

In the early 1970s, already notorious for the ferocity of motion pictures like *The Wild Bunch* and *Straw Dogs*, Sam Peckinpah appeared on the Johnny Carson show. He was in full apache mode: snarling, drunk, coked-up in fringed buckskin, boots, cowboy shirt, and— the contrary Noël Coward touch—tortoise shell cigarette holder. A mega-church preacher man had preceded him, one of the amiable big mouths talking up Christ, born-again-ness, and other soon-to-be cliches of the Christian Right. Peckinpah, listing in his chair, cocked an eye. When Johnny finally got his attention and asked a question, Peckinpah reared on the preacher man and growled: "Tell me, Reverend, how does it feel to be so goddamn *right?*"

◉◉◉

Inflammatory skepticism is elemental to the American poetic spirit. It's easy to question ethical opportunism and moral disingenuousness, less so to internalize skepticism and write out of it. McGrath distinguished two sorts of political poetry: "tactical" (which incites action) and "strategic" (which alters consciousness). Hamill's *Poets Against the War* does a little of both. The worst most contributors can be faulted for is writing bad poetry and indulging mere sensibility. My progressive politics align with theirs. A poem as broadside cry or public alarm has its use. If it exposes insanity in the polity, it raises consciousness. But if poets suppress ambiguity, generative vagueness, and destabilizing inquiry, they collude with the media circus we all criticize for its depredations on language. The media thrives and dominates because it insists on sentimental simplifications. If poets so indulge, they become their own enemy. I'd speculate that the best poem about our recent war may be written down the road by an ex-marine who, discovering a gift for words, offers complicated, equivocal witness authenticated by experience. I imagine a poem of painfully divided, uncertain feelings.

Then there's this. The nice idioms cultivated and encouraged in the hothouses of writing programs are inadequate to the worst (and best) of experience. Some poets write almost as proxies for past poets who had a fuller formal, rhetorical range. One piece in *Poets Against the War*, after stating the occasion ("Early in the day reports said our planes / had bombed a wedding in a distant country"), comes round to this: "It was exactly the sort of thing which in a Greek play / would initiate a sequence of events / that turns inexorably back to bite / the hand that set it into motion." This is shadow-boxing—there's no resistance. Adrienne Rich, Carolyn Kizer, and C. K. Williams contribute good, insinuating poems driven by mature political feeling and soundness of craft. But there are also instances of begging the question ("For a poet, whose morality and word are identities"), sticky nature allegory ("When a dead tree falls in a forest / it often falls into the arms of a living tree"), and pat sentimentalism ("Rain falls like the / tears of the bereaved").

In a sense, the poems can't win for losing. Many are preacher man poems hollered at the choir. A good holler clears the air. But I suspect that more than a few writers know in their hearts how ineffectual poetry is in the American polity. My quarrel, at any rate, is with the quality of the cry. I don't think poets should speak as if they're goddamn right. One says of her daughter's impatience with political talk: "like Achilles, / she stalks off to her room." To suggest that the Achilles who lives in the Western imagination is in any way comparable to a moody modern teenager is at best trivializing (and unfair to the girl), at worst as vulgarly indecorous as the remark of the American officer who said of Al Queda's terrorist network: "These are the kinds of guys who want a one-way ticket to Allah." And you don't denounce dehumanization by dehumanizing your subject. One writer speaks of the "robotic eyes" of American pilots. Maybe we should carve THEY HAD ROBOTIC EYES on the grave markers of poet flyboys like James Dickey, Richard Hugo, Harvey Shapiro, Howard Nemerov, and that unfeeling trainer of automatons, Randall Jarrell.

2003

"Baby Sweetness Blew His Cool Again"

(James Schuyler)

It's September 1958, and James Schuyler, who started writing art criticism in 1955 and would continue until 1975, is visiting Leland Bell's studio for an *Art News* profile. Bell, of the generation of Milton Resnick and Robert De Niro, Sr., is a familiar, polemical character in the New York art scene. He draws the figure at a time when Abstract Expressionism is still very much on people's minds though Pop, in its morosely naughty way, will soon break up everybody's party. The day of Schuyer's visit, Bell's working on a sketch of Rubens' *Allegory of the Outbreak of War*, which he has seen in the Pitti Palace. Schuyler's art writing has a certain affect: exact, measured in its enthusiasms, responsive to the sensuousness of line and structure. He reckons that Bell has been working on this particular drawing for months not to produce a finished work but "as a means of exploring Rubens' composition, to trace, if not to solve, the mystery." Schuyler's poems move that way: even when writing as a voluptuary, especially of the green and growing world, he doesn't linger too long on an object or effect. What matters is the tracery, anti-eloquent, light-handed, gestural. Some poets write about art because it's a dummy set-up that lets them state or test notions about the work of poetry. The alignments between Schuyler's poetry and art writing are too plumb to be accidental. In Bell's pictures he sees "passion, largeness, openness: A lot of the struggle is inward, in the cultivation of a scrupulous and discerning eye." That's his own eye:

> *A cardinal*
> *Passes like a flying tulip, alights and nails the green day*
> *Down. One flame in a fire of sea-soaked, copper-fed wood:*
> *A red that leaps from green and holds it there.*
>
> "Hymn to Life"

Listen to what I pay attention to, his art writing tells us, and you will learn to read my poems.

◉◉◉

How could I have known in 1963, when my senior English teacher used *Reader's Digest* articles to teach us speed reading—skate your finger like a polygraph needle down the center of the page—that I'd dust off the technique years later to get through the letters of a poet whose poetry I've admired so much for so long? After fifty pages of Schuyler's recently published letters, I practically gave up, they are so syrupy with kissy gossip, daily weather patterns, his amours and those of friends, his (literary, musical, pictorial, movie-going, culinary) tastes, what Fairfield and Frank and John and Kenneth are up to these days and O the way they do the things they do. The trivia seemed to clutter the space where an inner life should be, until I realized that it *was* his inner life, or a major dynamic of it anyway. His skittish letters, frilly with goodwill and at times giddily obscene—Schuyler seldom settles into the aroused ruminations of a Wallace Stevens or Hart Crane—are really reports from a fragile being who functioned best at the margin of things but who possessed the sturdiness and resolve to write a lot of superb poetry in his 67 years of life. The nonstop name-dropping, though, can induce a kind of mild food disgust.

In a brief stretch of letters in the mid-1960s, Schuyler mentions Raoul Walsh's 1936 picture *Klondike Annie* starring Mae West, Michael McClure's play *Billy the Kid*, Xavier Cugat, Emannuelle Khan (a fashion designer), Arlene Francis, Ernest Thompson Seton (co-founder of the Boy Scouts), Charles Ives, Margaret Fuller, John Garfield, and Ferruccio Busoni. Enough already? The poems are another matter, or a confluent matter: in them the days' trivia and culture-archiving become life essences. The this and that delirium begins to seem one demonstration (or symptom) of a mania which in its pathological expressions caused Schuyler great soul pain in his life. Now I realize I'm speed reading ten pages but then slow feeding on ten more then pausing over a few, and I get the sense that *he's* reading *me*, my patience, sensibility, and low tolerance for culture-vulturing. His letters expose the askew assumptions readers develop when they admire a poet before knowing anything about his character. In any event, the voice of the letter writer gets eventually confounded with the poet whose offerings I've fed on for so many years, wry or piercing about life's more dreadful moments, catty, erudite, fussily ecstatic about gardens and flowers—a voice that seems more exhalation than utterance. He camps it up more in the letters than the poems. He becomes Jimmy the fag, Jimmy the (sort of) dandified flâneur, the amateur botanist who falls in love with roses and writes about others' affairs with the terrier snappiness of a society columnist.

◉◉◉

Good descriptive poems are like perfumes made tactile. When I first lived in San Francisco in the late 1960s, the floral medicinals that dripped in the air, especially in heavy fog or after rains, drove me crazy—eucalyptus, star jasmine, mock orange, pittosporum. The other day, walking with a friend new to town, I picked things along the way: eucalyptus buttons, camphor leaves, medlar and lemon blossoms, the Scotch broom that Leopardi (whom Schuyler translated) wrote about in "*La ginestra*," and held them up for her to smell. "You're *erheben*-ing!" she said. It's German (she explained) for raising or lifting but suggests something selected and held up, singled out. It's what a woodworker might do, or Rembrandt. Schuyler's best poems do that. Bittersweet Jimmy, the only poet of the bunch that included Ashbery, O'Hara, Koch, and Guest whom we feel we can call by his nickname, so elegant, impressionable, and sadly manic is the voice of the poems, likes to *erheben*:

> *I love*
> *this garden in all its moods,*
> *even under its wintry coat*
> *of salt hay, or now,*
> *in October, more than*
> *half gone over: here*
> *a rose, there a clump*
> *of aconite.*
>
> —"Korean Mums"

Description isn't just a way of telling us what the world looks like, of making what Pound called "accurate reports." It expresses the feeling a poet has for the existence of things. Like Hardy, Frost, and Edward Thomas, Schuyler is essentially a scenic poet. For all of them description is the psyche's graphic: words bite like acids into the given world's copper plate. Those older poets are scenic in patterned, rhetorically constructed ways, and the constructedness is part of the pleasure. Schuyler is more combustively casual. His way of describing flowers or city streets or interiors is like a display of neural firings haphazardly networking with other clustered firings, every observation barely or lightly tethered to the one before or after. The congested, antsy skittishness we hear in the letters becomes in the poems a technique of elided disclosures, and whenever Schuyler makes statements of consequence, they sound like accidents not essences, accents incidental to the drift of the lines. The poems are often runny and loosely structured, so his formal task is to hold the cognitive networks together in some sort of elastic pattern or to carom scenic elements off each other in a foxy way. "The Crystal Lithium"—he wrote Kenneth Koch that he took the title off a postcard, "an old-timey spa, somewhere in the south Kaintuck, I think"—opens thus:

> *The smell of snow, stinging in nostrils as the wind lifts it from a beach*
> *Eye-shuttering, mixed with sand, or when snow lies under the street*
> *lamps*
>   *and on all*
> *And the air is emptied to an uplifting gassiness*
> *That turns lungs to winter waterwings, buoying, and the bright white*
> *night*
> *Freezes in sight a lapse of waves, balsamic, salty, unexpected.*

The poem's skeleton—an almanac of months and weathers—is rubbery enough to tolerate impacted perceptions, daffy facts, and twisty syntax, all in service to a report on "that which is, which is beyond / Happiness or love or mixed with them or more than they or less, unchanging change." He veers this way and that, inside poems long and short, early and late, Fatso Jimmy with the weight problem staying light on his feet. In 1956, putting out in four days a dozen exhibition reviews while on the tranquilizer Miltown since a manic episode several years earlier, he tells a critic-correspondent: "No one takes his lightness more seriously than I." He relishes the fact that New York bums commonly address strangers not as "Bud" or "Pal" but as "Jimmy."

◉◉◉

The dog returns to its bowl. The letters' gossip occasionally puts me off my food, but in the poems I lap it up. And even the letters deliver unexpected goods: one sitting, I'm exasperated by the chit-chat, next sitting I'm caught up by the apparent breeziness of his day-to-day life. (He doesn't talk much about his mental illness, though his Payne Whitney poems are among his best.) The letters' salt-and-pepper facts about starlets, operetta singers, comic strip characters, and the like, are essential to the "play" in his life, to his conversation with life's come-and-go needs, which is one of the intimacies poets' letters disclose. His self-aware jollity and shared delights can be very winning. In a poem from the 1960s, "Dining Out with Doug and Frank," I feel I'm reading a typically Jimmy-esque account of life lived at its nerve ends, life so eventful in its seeming uneventfulness that it makes me feel I've been sleepwalking in my own life. In the poems generally, the newsy tidbits and cultural stuffing and Jimmy's ongoing state of being, plus today's prevailing winds or rain, while they seem merely to occur to him in process of composition, all get cannily textured and tissued together. The poems blend—aspirate, really—herky-jerky rhythms and honeyed tones, fluid utterances and broken continuities. Schuyler spreads his seemingly rambling, wistful, fact-hounding, "Ain't-this-something?" manner across the picture plane of the poem with a sly evenness. In "Afterward" he spreads out these: a spilled bottle of pills; a Diet Pepsi he's drinking; his new Olivetti portable; a fire he started by smoking in bed, the subsequent third-degree burns and hospitalization; then this: "when I came out // feeling great wham / a nervous breakdown: four / weeks in another hospital."

◎◎◎

Jimmy the Religioso? Until he converted to Episcopalianism not long before he died, Schuyler was a nonbeliever, though he liked to joke that he was a "crypto-catholic." In "The Morning of the Poem" he says: "I can live, it seems, without religion, though I have never wanted to." The poems hold up physical reality, its sheer materiality, as if it were a glazed spiritual expanse, a thinly spread condensation of some other energy state. His religious passion, if I can call it that—one of his strangest letters, written in 1985 to Ann Porter, recounts a visionary episode in which he felt protected by the "wind in the wings of your words"—is the constant awareness of a simultaneousness of actions. He was unstoppably eager for what the *world* offered *him*. His apparently naïve scrumming of this and that was actually a fiction for binding the poems together, to keep them from flying apart from their own vividness. They would otherwise have become (like useless gossip) random facts skimming gamely and fecklessly across the surfaces of things.

> *A tennis ball is served*
> *A horsefly vanishes.*
> *A smoking cigarette.*
> *A day (so many and so few)*
> *dies down a hardened sky*
> *and leaves are lap-held notebook leaves*
> *discriminated barely*
> *in leaves no longer layered.*
>
> —"Song"

Schuyler's poetry is like attention deficit disorder turned to lyric advantage, a way of weaving the vapors and bulks of sensation and thought into a now silky, now gravelly meditative squirminess, a repining restlessness that keeps tossing him back upon the world's bosom: "Life, it seems, explains nothing about itself."

❂❂❂

What Schuyler wrote about the paintings of Robert De Niro, Sr. that "the world presents a continuous skin to our sight, first as color and mass, then as feature and line," describes the responsiveness of his poems, which tease out his preoccupation with interrupted surfaces as well as interrupted writing and lives and psychological balance. The preoccupation is the source of his melancholy. One of his themes is the melancholy of distance, of places (and faces, objects, weathers) recalled as if they were immanent presences: poems that are, as de Kooning described his pictures, "slipping glimpses," sequential moments when uncalled-for events shuffle into the current instant, "Why *that* / dinner table is / *this* breakfast table." Here he is, making breakfast in a friend's house: "Let me tell you / that this weekend Sunday / morning in the country / fills my soul / with tranquil joy." The merry blending of Wordsworth and William Carlos Williams apart, his scanning of the morning's events and sensations restores to him the previous evening's gossip, a shopping expedition, today's favorite shrub (bayberry), the cat that killed the goldfinch, the healthfulness of coffee(!), and his desire for a long swim. But the chain-linking of events can break: "Discontinuity / in all we see and are: / the same, yet change, / change, change." The effort of the work is to find and make a pattern that holds together the uncountable and unaccountable data experience floods our way: to make of hazard a pattern of sense. In "The Morning of the Poem," written while he was staying at Fairfield Porter's house on Great Spruce Head Island in Maine—he lived with the Porter family for eleven years, in Southampton and Maine—he keeps rounding back to the melancholy of distance: How is the wind in New York tonight, and where is that mountain I think I see here on the Island, and *somewhere* are dunes, surf, and a four-poster bed. The shifting sounds of the poems can at any moment drop him into a melancholy so profound that we forget the sassy ironies and kitsch-cuddling he sometimes indulges in, a darkness he's lost to until his wits seine him back to himself, to hope in life and writing.

◉◉◉

I don't like "painterly" poetry, the sort that pants after beauty, drooling a little, *delicately*, while calling attention to the exquisite sensibility we are all fortunate enough to behold. The painterliness that matters in poetry lies in a structured suppleness that hums in response to what Cézanne called the "little sensation" that physical reality stirs in us. Words as merely self-aware marvels and wonderments make for decadence. Poetry is patterning, something made *thus* and *thus*, words shape-shifting into a surprised and surprising sense that conjures the amazements of the ordinary. Schuyler secretes the scene as he goes along:

> *Traffic sounds and*
> *bells resound in silver clangs*
> *the hour, a tune, my friend*
> *Pierrot. The violet hour:*
> *the grass is violent green.*
> *A weeping beech is gray,*
> *A copper beech is copper red.*
> *Tennis nets hang*
> *Unused in unused stillness.*
>
> —"Song"

This is painterly: it reimagines a shared reality as a tracery in consciousness, alarmed by feeling. Schuyler doesn't fashion a mental image as an art object positioned for our admiration but as something restlessly ambiguous, kneaded into the feeling tones of daily life. A poem has "depth" if it's rich in consequence within the actions and feeling zones of the poem itself and if it's contiguous and confluent with how we look at the world, how we live in and talk about it. Bland, suburban, academic (i.e., written according to internalized prescriptions or permissions) poetry can cause readers to carry starved values into their way of talking about the world. How the phenomenal world engages our attention, how it leads us through the here and now—these are Schuyler's subject and style. He liked Apollinaire's remark about poetry combining discipline with personality. Schuyler's discipline of seeing and writing was so casual as to seem no discipline at all. Leland Bell's reservation about Alberto Giacometti, whose work he loved, was that he made art look too hard. Schuyler made it look easy.

⊚⊚⊚

Physical letters, unlike email (easy street for artful dodgers and control freaks), bear a certain weight of personal moral residues. Even if cool or newsy or prankish in content, one knows that a hand folded the sheet and sealed the envelope, and in that hand lie a style and psychology more or less transparent. When gossip and name-dropping aren't inducing tedium, Schuyler's letters can be plaintively self-aware, funny, and prodigal. His crowded, fluttery, tic-cy mind sprints through experience, trying to make room, as he does in the poems, for *every little thing.* (We know from Justin Spring's biography of Porter that in person Jimmy could be manipulative, mooching, testy, and petulant.) He certainly knew that nothing is quite so boring as a description of one's pain, so he doesn't go on about his Vale of Soul-Making, the episodes of bipolar disorder and schizophrenia that started in 1951 and made his later years hell, and when he does, he decontaminates the chamber with send-up humor. Sometimes he tips his hand. In letters while hospitalized for several months in Vermont in 1971—"Baby Sweetness blew his cool again"—he records the incoherence and pain. In these choppy, piecemeal communiqués to the outside world (you always feel he's writing from an island, real like Manhattan or Great Spruce Head, or interiorized) we hear his purest genius, which runs just this side of word salad, a daintily controlled speed babble. When he's in his right mind, he's a seducer with a very acute eye. In one letter, after a list of I-do-this-I-do-that reports, he says "And so the days wear away." That could be a phrase from one of his poems, which like the letters braid with loping, stuttered urgency the trivial with the sublime. We hear about what he's writing, what's on TV ("I'm in the circular TV freak-out lounge," written during a hospital stay), how friends are doing, that "lilac" derives from a Persian word, what the latest stereo equipment goes for, and isn't Carly Simon great, but is she greater than Cat Stevens? The letters teem with generous tenderness towards others and the natural order, garlanded with little epiphanies of attention to nuance, to changes of mood or atmosphere. To Joe Brainard, who is minding the Porters' Southampton house, Schuyler stipulates that the begonias are best watered with a particular white enamel teapot to be found in the cupboard, then mentions his current passion for field grasses, especially Quaking Grass: "[It] makes the best 18th century trembler I ever saw look clunky. (Have you ever seen a trembler in motion? A piece of jewelry with some of the stones mounted on fine wires, so they quiver all the time.)" He's someone on whom, like Henry James's ideal artist, nothing is lost. He also knows the trouble it brings: "To live, to live! So natural and so hard."

❦❦❦

From early on, Schuyler was preoccupied with what he called an achieved style. Replying in 1954 to a remark by Porter about self-parody, he wrote: "It's often hard to say which flower [among poems by a contemporary] bloomed first, and whether one is wax. So much of art is an exercising of an achieved style—there are so many Monets I would like singly and together, without finding a special uniqueness in any of them. The uniqueness seems to me between the total work and the rest of the world." He separates this from manner, talking about artists, though it fits poets, too, who in their twenties and thirties contrive a signature manner they ride throughout their career. "I don't say their work is without merit, but I think it's mostly an achieved manner, and manner, en masse, makes for ennui." Compare the early 1951 "Salute" to "The Morning of the Poem" from the early 1980s to see how Schuyler cross-grains or sabotages what might have become an achieved manner. "Salute" is Mallarmé channeled through Crane. "The Morning of the Poem," less shambling than Schuyler's earlier long poem, "Hymn to Life" (written in the early 1970s), tests the boundaries of what he could already do, experimenting with patterns, tonal frequencies, and directed digressiveness. (De Kooning: "I have to keep changing in order to stay the same.") We all know poets who won't surprise us with a different sound because they've become habituated to a manner and the critical attention the manner attracts. If there's restlessness in such work, it's only wind rippling a pond—it doesn't kick up bottom sand. Schuyler could have settled into a manner of pleasurable flatline energy, engaging but responsive to experience in predictable ways. What saved him from the monotonous butcher-block whacking of, say, Lowell's *History* was a stylistic restlessness responsive to emotional and intellectual instability. A poem's "finish" depends on internal dynamics, not shellacked surfaces. "Style in art," he says of Proust, "is not a matter of study, practice, revision or refinement of diction (means) but of vision." This appears in a letter to John Button, a painter Schuyler met and fell for in the 1950s: "There is a line which you sometimes use which . . . if it's undesirable, it's because it gives off a look of 'finish', and a work should not look more finished than it intrinsically is." Schuyler was aware of his own sleight of hand gesturalism that exasperates some readers of his poetry and made of irresoluteness and uncertainty a chased "finish." So that I don't leave the impression that Schuyler the letter writer was a long beard, I have to quote the closing of one he sent to Button and Frank O'Hara: "I want to finish pricking out the silouette of my dick and am going to put lipstick on my sphincter so I can plant a nice kiss on the outside of this letter." The letters tumble together this kind of queered-up rowdiness with the wounded pleadings, lubricity, and droning darksome bittersweetness, the sugared vinegar, that we hear in the poems.

◉◉◉

The most excruciating and uncharacteristic letter is addressed to one Nancy Batie, a Vancouver woman about whom little is known but who by 1969 was a passionate, well-informed reader of Schuyler's work. (Breakdowns, hospitalizations, and migrations from one S.R.O. hotel to another resulted in very few letters from 1973-1979.) "Jimmy" vanishes in a jinn's vapor of politeness and formality that's unsettling because it's the kind of writing—stuffy self-explanatory exposition—that came least naturally to this man who wrote such wicked-smart art criticism. The sentences squirm with discomfort, weirdly formal, almost ventriloquist, composed by Herr Professor Schuyler. But he does give some things away. Defending his attic-clutter poems, he admits he's partial to art "where disparate elements form an entity" and that he especially likes Kurt Schwitters' collages, made of "commercial bits and 'found' pieces but which always compose a whole striking for its completeness." He doesn't so much talk about writing as he demonstrates what goes into making the poems, the agitated-ness and bemusement, the self-inventiveness and improvisations, the processual piecing together of this and that. It's clear that his writerly ambition was the one Baudelaire attributed to the modern artist: to find the eternal in the transitory. The Batie letter was found among John Ashbery's papers. Schuyler wrote but never sent it.

2006

Brag, Sweet Tenor Bull

(Basil Bunting)

In 1964, during his daily commute to a job writing a financial page and humdrum copy for the Newcastle *Evening Chronicle*, the only regular work this man as old as the century could find, from a phrase ("Brag, sweet tenor bull") written many years earlier and a remembered scene fifty years past, Basil Bunting began to construct the contents of his life: childhood (with sweetheart), vagabonding, sailing, espionage, scholarship, poetry and music, compounded by meditations on history, Northumbrian history in particular, its saints, heroes and kings. By 1965 he had finished *Briggflatts* (published in *Poetry* in January 1966), his first work after a thirteen-year silence. In a later interview he recalled a springtime scene: "It occurred to me, at once, nobody had noticed the bull has a *tenor* voice. . . . He bellows in the most melodious tenor. In spring, the bull does in fact, if he's with the cows, dance, on the tip of his toes, part of the business of showing off . . . to demonstrate to the cows what an indispensable creature he is." Proper to the sort of poet he was, Bunting's description contains the man, his intellectual passion and scampish sexual relish for the particulars of physical reality. It also bespeaks the sort of poetry he wrote. Poetry should be like song and dance: sound and movement make its meaning. Experience is content *and* formal drive. "You can't write about anything," he said many times in many ways, "unless you've experienced it." As bare anecdote, experience was nil: "You don't set out to make a poem of your experience. You set out to make a shape. A shape of sounds." During that thirteen-year silence, during which he sometimes earned his bread proofreading suburban train timetables, seedsmen's catalogs, and electoral lists, one of his few literary contacts was Louis Zukofsky. In a 1964 letter to Zukofsky, grieving over the death of the teenage son from his first marriage who had been living in America and whom Bunting hadn't seen in many years, he wrote: "In the grave's narrow slot / they lie: we rot." In that same letter he roughs out ideas for new poems, one of them rather long.

I first read Bunting in the early 1980s. I'd just begun teaching poetry workshops, which seemed then (and still) quite abstract, and was astonished to hear young writers speak (as they still do) of "getting a poem out of" some experience. Find a juicy orange and squeeze it dry. *Briggflatts*, and in a less obsessive way Bunting's odes, were models, for anyone who cared, of poetry as a shapely form of feeling, of sounds set into memorable patterns. Like Lorine Niedecker, whose work he much admired, and Zukofsky, Bunting had already been shoved to the margins of the mid-century canon. Anthologists, who can literary taste like chopped pineapple (with, like pineapple producers, an eye on market share), didn't dig him, or checked him off as a Poundling. My 1983 edition of *The Norton Anthology of English Poetry* contains no Bunting. The most recent two volume *Norton Anthology of Modern and Contemporary Poetry* gives Bunting five pages (two lyrics and Part I of *Briggflatts*). Hart Crane gets 43 pages, Robert Graves six, Melvin Tolson ten. Who would infer from that brokering that Bunting wrote one of the great long poems of the last century, easily the match of *The Bridge* (included whole in the *Norton*). Bunting isn't easy, but neither is Crane (or Tolson for that matter). Bunting may be an acquired taste, but once acquired, it sets an intoxicating measure; thenceforth one flinches at the mention of, say, Elizabeth Bishop as "a poet's poet." The Bunting local pokes along: Fulcrum's *Collected Poems* appeared in England in 1968, was reprinted by Oxford in

1978, and crossed over here in Moyer Bell's 1985 edition. In 1994 Oxford produced a *Complete Poems* that included a dozen uncollected odes and a batch of translations and imitations, now available here from New Directions.

I read Bunting's work, from the 1935 "Villon" to the spare lyrics of the 1960s and 1970s included in "The Second book of Odes," as a matrix for *Briggflatts*. It's a bias unfair to the poet and the poems, but *Briggflatts* has such monstruous music, silky-airy to rocky-rancid, that it rises from the other poems the way the mountain range of Gog and Magog at world's end erupts in the episode of Alexander's legendary adventures. *Briggflatts*, at over 400 lines, is an epic as Pound defined it, a poem containing history, containing, first of all, personal history, which is to say the forging of subjectivity. It also involves seventeen heroes and twelve plot lines outpouched with various cultures—Anglo-Saxon, early Christian, Mediterranean. Like epic, it's all transitionless foreground and cares nothing for psychology. The matter of Alexander lies on the same narrative plane with a Basil Bunting young and old and the Norwegian King Eric Bloodaxe's eighth century defeat at the battle of Stainmore and interstellar time.

We now can hear Bunting talking over our shoulders while we read him. Peter Makin, Bunting's best critic (whose 1992 *Bunting: The Shaping of his Verse* is still available, but only in England, and only for a jaunty $125), has edited and annotated lectures Bunting gave at Newcastle University in the early 1970s, *Basil Bunting on Poetry*, where Bunting sets out his version of the history of English poetry, lorded by Wyatt, Spenser, and Wordsworth. The lectures bluster with the self-effacing contentiousness of a man whose knowledge of the tradition was worked up outside academic hierarchies. Bunting, who never graduated college, is a wily master of the recusation: "I don't deserve your attention because I can't claim special knowledge in these matters, *but* . . ." And he protests almost too much. He says, several times in several ways, in the lectures and in interviews from his later years, that he's "scarcely ever concerned with myself at all in verse." In *Briggflatts* (not to speak of the erotic odes with their desert-bloom beauty) his personal self, even more specifically his Northumbrian Quaker self, is the foundation on which history's layers are snugly mortared.

In his poetry Bunting never cared about endearing himself to an audience, and in the talks he relishes breaking tablets of law. Contesting what he takes to be the Standard Version of the canon, he declares that Chaucer is *not* the father of English poetry. He's carping at a commonplace, I suppose, but who would bother going to the mat over the issue? In the Bunting Version it's Sir Thomas Wyatt, or "Wyat" as he spells it, who deserves the title, because he returned to the sources of poetry in court dance and song, and, while knowledgeable in French, Spanish, and Italian poetry (as was Bunting, who also had Persian), remained "astonishingly simple and very English." Bunting built on Pound's assertion that poets should compose by musical phrase, not in sequence of the metronome—"[T]here was no substitute for music as a guide. A Poet must write by ear."—and his historical views bear this out. It's no surprise that someone who in his poetry was so intent on dissolving the membrane cellophaning sound from sense should decry the moment in the sixteenth century when poets "lost touch with music" and replaced musicality with the rule of neatness, a monotony of wit, syntax, and cadence. "If a poet starts counting syllables and heeding the rules prosodists invent," he said, "writing verses becomes a pedantic game on a par with crossword puzzles." From the early odes through *Briggflatts*, Bunting's sounds owe more to the sweet irregular sonorities of Wyatt than to the fussy economies of subsequent poets.

Though he benefited much from his association with Pound, Bunting wasn't a Pound-ish internationalist. He insisted not only on his Englishness but on the provincial Northumbrian character of the sounds he made. He also insisted, like Hopkins, that his poetry was grounded in common speech. Of "Villon" (the 1925 poem occasioned by Bunting's realization that the lock-up where he woke after a binge and tussle with French police was the same room where 500 years earlier Villon was interrogated) Makin says: "Sound's form is the entity-maker." The poem also flashes Bunting's sharper edges:

> *Remember, imbeciles and wits,*
> *sots and ascetics, fair and foul,*
> *young girls with little tender tits,*
> *that DEATH is written over all.*
>
> *Worn hides that scarcely clothe the soul*
> *they are so rotten, old and thin,*
> *or firm and soft and warm and full,*
> *fellmonger Death gets every skin.*

Good music of any kind can be difficult, with jangling tone rows (Schoenberg puts in an appearance in *Briggflatts*) and complex chromatics. Bunting wanted words to be related closely to music, but not only in sound. *Briggflatts* is constructed as a five-movement-plus-coda Baroque sonata. And line for line, whether composing in the hammer-and-anvil meters of early English poetry, writing feathery Campion-esque airs, or chanting rolling hollers out of Whitman (whom he admired for his ability to "hold verse together without a rigid or repetitive pattern"), Bunting shaped for each occasion a compelling musicality that had its own economy, that budgeted expressiveness against restraint, tunefulness against sense. I get the drift but don't take Bunting entirely at his word when he says that poetry's meanings arise entirely out of the shape of sounds, that "what poetry professes to tell us is scarcely relevant." The lines in *Briggflatts* that resulted from those in the Zukofsky letter, "In the grave's slot / he lies. We rot," make pile-driving music, yes, but the absolutist thump of its sense tells us, as it told the grieving Bunting, something.

The supple dramatic voices of earlier poems like "The Well of

Lycopolis," "Chomei at Toyama," and "The Spoils," owed much to Bunting's father, who read long passages of Wordsworth aloud to his young son. The gene string for his ventriloquist gifts runs through Browning, Hardy, and Pound. He esteemed Wordsworth as "the most skillful, and the most complex, of narrative poets in English," while acknowledging Yeats's complaint that Wordsworth restored common speech to the language of poetry but ignored syntax, which, he reminds us, was Yeats's own means of coining a poetic equivalent of modern speech. Bunting's anointings and chastisements, like any poet's, defend his own practice and measure his own ambitions. *Briggflatts*, with its clenched, compounded storylines, is a denser and more robustly inflected narrative than anything I'm aware of in Wordsworth, and its methods are different. Wordsworth sleeves plot inside plot, voice inside voice; Bunting crunches them, and his version (or reinvention) of plain speech shrinks normalizing grammatical tissue to a very tight seam. Wordsworth is more familiar, casual, diffuse. He unscrolls a world of sheeted facts before us. Bunting chops out facts like wartime bulletins. Subjectivity is so deeply socketed in *Briggflatts* that we're aware we're reading a mega-lyric (subjectivity doesn't have to announce its presence) and because it's a nonchronological narrative poem without transitions, rhythmic variety is crucial. Different materials are marked by changes in texture and tempo. In one of the poem's several instances of poetic self-declaration Bunting shifts from a bloody scene of predation in the natural and human orders—"I hear Aneurin number the dead and rejoice, / being adult male of a merciless species"—to this sweet tune:

> *It is time to consider how Domenico Scarlatti*
> *condensed so much music into so few bars*
> *with never a crabbed turn or congested cadence,*
> *never a boast or a see-here.*

As a gloss on Bunting's procedures, that's accurate much of the time (and a tonic for young poets) but doesn't completely align with the poem's dynamics, which sometimes do indeed call attention to themselves. But that comes, I think, with the sort of narrative Bunting chose to write. Wordsworth's narratives are veils-on-veils; *Briggflatts* has no transparencies.

Bunting was a tough-minded secular realist but was raised a Quaker, attended Quaker school, went to meeting house (in the village of Brigflatts), and knew much scripture by heart. He wasn't pious or devout in the way Herbert or Hopkins was and showed no interest in the intervention of Christ in history. "I am fundamentally averse to acts of faith," he said. "Faith being belief contrary to the available evidence." He described himself as a sort of pantheist, and his poetry feels driven by pre-Christian energies. He was in any event fascinated by animism and its expressions, from Paleozoic cave art to the life art of Francis of Assisi, whom he associated with Northumberland's early Christian missionaries. He also perceived an affinity between Saint Francis and Arab ways of living—Bunting spent some years during and after World War II in Persia—not through any connections of religious practice or saintliness but because, as Makin puts it, "the Middle Eastern view defies security, and materialism in general, for something it values better." Bunting lived his life that way, by intent or default, lived it (like Villon) at headlong pitch, improvising his livelihood and taking to sea alone for long periods. The Quaker in him suspected materialism of every shape and variety and certainly never benefited from its capitalist rewards.

Briggflatts inquires into the physical reality of history where "[T]oday's posts are piles to drive into the quaggy past / on which impermanent palaces balance." Matter—clods, clover, marble, iron, rat, bull, bird—is the charter and archive of Bunting's religiousness. This from a 1977 interview:

> *There is a possibility of a kind of reverence for the whole of creation which I feel we all ought to have in our bones, a kind of pantheism.*

If the word "God" is to have any use it must include everything. The only way to know anything is to consider yourself a student of histology, finding out as much as carefully controlled commonsense can find out about the world. In so doing, you will be contributing to the histology of God.

Histology is the study of cells, and *Briggflatts* is a cellular agglomerate of memories so deeply fixed in matter—in the stone he and Peggy Greenbank (his companion at meeting house) lie on as children, spider floss that downed her cheek, Stainmore's bloody soil, dung cakes peddled by prototypical capitalist merchants, figs, starfish, scones, and flesh—that it reads like an ardent taxonomy of the physical world calculated, however, by non-material astronomical reckonings. All of *Briggflatts'* action is finally suspended in interstellar light; knowledge and affects are subject to temporal delay. When Bunting was released from prison in 1919 after serving six months as a conscientious objector—*after* the Armistice: such obstinacy and conviction are the temperamental bedrock of the poetry—he didn't return to Briggflatts and Peggy but pitched himself into his life as a poet until fifty-odd years later, when in his poem he remembers all the histories encoded in that love. The great love of Peggy that "lies fifty years dead," is reckoned by the speed of the light of Betelgeuse ("Sailors pronounce *Betelgeuse* 'Beetle juice,' and so do I"), which takes fifty years to reach us. What binds the poem's cellular consistency is sex, the slowworm (or blindworm, a sometimes limbless, small-eyed lizard) that slinks through the poem's different locales.

Then is Now. The star you steer by is gone,
its tremulous thread spun in the hurricane
spider floss on my cheek; light from the zenith
spun when the slowworm lay in her lap
fifty years ago.

Wheat lies in excrement. Seeds thrive in the corruption of their flowers. The poet Aneirin counts men slain by Northumbria's conquerors several hundred years ago. Bunting sails south toward Italy. St. Cuthbert converts the Anglos. The poem, like the slow-worm, migrates constantly one to another, season to season, migrates like the poet, who "lies with one to dream of another," which describes the essential restlessness of the imagination. *Briggflatts* occupies an intensified present, living itself into the past and change: "What can he, changed, tell / her, changed, perhaps dead?" It's history all at once and comes closer than any poem I know to realizing what William James said is impossible:

> *Can we realize for an instant what a cross-section of all existence at a definite point in time would be? While I talk and the flies buzz, a sea-gull catches a fish at the mouth of the Amazon, a tree falls in the Adirondack wilderness, a man sneezes in Germany, a horse dies in Tartary, and twins are born in France.*

Briggflatts is also a directory of tropes for the identity of the poet, music maker but also stone-cutter, who measures and "lays his rule / at a letter's edge," his rhythm-section mallet in sync with the natural order, timed "to a lark's twitter," and whose language marks mortality against the erosive constancy of nature. (The entire poem is haunted by Hardy's line in "During Wind and Rain": "Down their carved names the raindrop plows.") Alexander's journey to the end of the known world, a story Bunting lifted from a Persian version of the medieval *Legend of Alexander*, is the story of a modern moral intelligence that has to traverse the most vile sort of commercialism, shit-mongering, in order to test itself against nature's sublime power. As wheat thrives in excrement, human aspiration has to wade through excrement. Bunting had his musical model for poetry—"Poetry and music are both patterns of sound drawn on a background of time"—but he had a graphic one, too, in the Lindisfarne Gospels, a collection of medieval illuminated manuscripts where image and word are elaborately plaited and interwoven. As freighted as *Briggflatts* is with physicality, it's made of words, of abstractions. Bunting believed that poetry was truly realized only when sounded out by the human voice. "Poetry lies dead on the page," he said in an interview, "until some voice brings it to life, just as music, on the stave, is no more than instructions to the player." He described the art of the Lindisfarne Gospels as "utterly abstract, and it is complex to an extraordinary degree, without ever losing its unity and proportion." As abstract as music, I'd add, though lacking music's immediate sensational effects. The Lindisfarne manuscripts, like *Briggflatts*, strike our senses all at once, as a solidified pattern that breaks down into graphic increments which slink and fuse and stream one into another. Details from the Gospels reproduced in the collection of talks are like a hologram of the interleaved complications of *Briggflatts*. And like everything in this elegiac poem, the more complete the presence, the keener the sensation of loss:

> *Tortoise deep in dust or*
> *muzzled bear capering*
> *punctuate a text whose initial*
> *lost in Lindisfarne plaited lines,*
> *stands for discarded love.*

The *Collected Poems* Bunting put together in 1968, "written here and there now and then over forty years and four continents," ran some 130 pages, excluding the translations and imitations he called "Overdrafts." He was hard on himself and was, he said, a great friend of the wastebasket. What's remarkable is that the irregular textures and muscular rhythms of Bunting's language changed very little throughout his career. The Anglo-Saxon sounds and jammed-up syntax of a 1932 ode ("Mesh cast for mackerel / by guess and the sheen's tremor") ring again clearly in an ode from 1975 ("Stones indeed sift to sand, oak / blends with saints' bones").

And from start to finish he's preoccupied with instability, decay, loss, and restoration. ("Look how clouds dance / under the wind's wing, and leaves / delight in transience.") Bunting's work isn't just thematically all of a piece; it *sounds* like one sustained music. One reason for the relatively small number of poems he preserved was his conviction that poetry be about, and written from, experience.

> *Secret, solitary, a spy, he gauges*
> *lines of Flemish horse*
> *hauling beer, the angle, obtuse, a slut's blouse draws on her chest,*
> *counts beat against beat, bus conductor*
> *against engine against whelks against*
> *the pedal, Tottenham Court Toad, decodes*
> *thunder, scans*
> *porridge bubbling, pipes clanking.*

This is a fair self-description, and not only because Bunting liked his pint, spent much time alone, worked for British intelligence in post–World War II Teheran, and had an eye for the girls, but because it conforms to the evidence of the consciousness in the poems, one of practical intelligence and aching appetites which sees the palpable world as a musical system of designs that can include illuminated gospels along with that slut's blouse.

2005

Get Chianti

(Hayden Carruth)

On the Porch

I went to find Hayden Carruth when I was living in Vermont in the mid-1970s and he was running his small farmstead, patching together a living with literary hack work, haying, tractor repair, barn-building and any other money-eking enterprise, on a hill outside Johnson about 40 miles from me. When I phoned in advance, his was the quietest telephone voice I'd ever heard; each sentence seemed to fade toward silence as it closed. His best poems are like that, soft-spoken, plain, even when the emotional signature is hacked or burnt into hardwood, and they possess absolute candor about everything. He's the least self-censoring person I know, his honesty embedded in Camus' writings, which were foundational for him. So there we were one summer afternoon sitting on the small porch of the modest house he kept with his then wife Rose Marie. He's chewing on his pipe stem, looking off into the distance. He *gazed*; his conversation seemed aimed at some elsewhere. He lived so deeply inside himself that he makes the oily, after-dinner-speaker-type poets we're all familiar with seem like carnie shills. When I pulled out my cigarettes, he cadged one.

—A little whiskey would go well with this.

So there we were, smoking Luckies, sipping Jim Beam or some

other corny liquor, when a typical country Vermont oil-burning junker too large to fit in most people's living rooms rattled past.

—Glad I don't have to earn money fixing those things anymore.

He wasn't talking about a summer job. He'd done everything except teach, which he did only as temporary gigs until 1979, when he went to a professorship at Syracuse University. He called himself a hack because he'd done, for money, just about every sort of writing and editing, working in the cowshed we could see from the porch. I asked about the stream that ran near his house.

—You're a Vermonter, you should know it's not a stream, it's a *brook*.

—I'm not a Vermonter. I'm from South Philadelphia, you know that. We'd call it a creek, a *crik*.

—Doesn't matter. You should know anyway.

We talked for hours. He loved Dryden's dramatic lyrics and put me on to the poetry of Paul Goodman, whom I knew from the frantic 1960s only as a social critic. We smoked up a storm. Smoking cigarettes was one of my greatest pleasures and had been one of his. Back then he went through 20 pipes a day. In his autobiography, *Reluctantly,* he describes an uncle smoking: "He would talk and exhale smoke at the same time, so that the smoke came out every which way, as if it were the ectoplasmic embodiment of his language."

Panic

One pick-up job was his stint as editor of *Poetry* in 1950. He was proud he never kept a poet waiting more than five weeks for an answer. But he riled the board by revamping and amping up things with more challenging poems and feistier prose, so within a year he was out. He loved Chicago for its jazz and blues and could still run down the sidemen on many sessions but was also agoraphobic and not cut out for cities. He didn't like having too many people around and suffered disabling panic attacks and other agonizing psychological ailments that afflicted him but lived in the shadow of the major one—suicidal depression.

California

Early 1990s. He visits me in California. We drive over an old stage road to the ocean; along the way, while he blows cigarette smoke out the window like a teenager, he asks the names of trees, grasses, flowers, stuff he'd never seen. He points to a shrub with smoky blue flowers.

—What's that thing?

—Ceanothus. They call it California lilac.

—But it's not lilac. Doesn't look anything like lilac.

That night I cook minestrone and joke about how Italians cook vegetables to kingdom come.

—So did my grandmother. Cooked the hell out of 'em. I do the same. This is good.

Italian Restaurant

Mid-1990s and he's back in California to read at Stanford, where I was then teaching. We plan to meet for dinner prereading, and I find him at the bar of a trendy Italian restaurant in Palo Alto. He's retired from Syracuse and lives in Munnsville, an upstate New York hamlet briefly famous for a fratricide documented in the movie *Brother's Keeper*. We haven't seen each other in a few years and make small talk until the bartender drifts over and asks our pleasure.

—Get Chianti (the only red Hayden seems to drink).

—I'll have a Prosecco.

—(Bartender) Sorry, sir, we don't have that.

—How can you call yourself an Italian restaurant and not serve Prosecco?

—Right! That's telling him! You have to make yourself heard. Bartender! Bring this man a glass of Chianti!

At dinner with his vivacious wife Joe-Anne, and looking much older since his last visit, he's telling a story and trying to set it in context.

—That was about six months after I killed myself, right, Joe-Anne?

They both laugh. He's referring to one of his suicide attempts, the time he came closest, in 1988, when he took every pill in his possession, and there were many indeed to take. His first knowledge of the suicidal impulse, involving more smoke, is recorded in *Reluctantly*. As a twelve-year-old sitting on a riverbank with a flirty girl who challenges him to toss away the pack he's smoking, he throws it into the river. The image of the pack falling and floating away lived powerfully in him ever after: "Why didn't I pitch myself after it and dash out my brains on the rocks below?" It would have been that easy, even then.

On a Walk

As part of his visit, Stanford has arranged a TV interview. The morning of the taping, he tells Joe-Anne he's stepping out for a little air. The event coordinator arrives to pick him up but Hayden's nowhere in sight. The coordinator waits, Joe-Anne waits, the studio waits. After an hour, everyone (except Joe-Anne, who knows her man does whatever his spirit tells him to do) is frantic. Should they put out a missing persons report? Will they need a helicopter? Will the TV affiliate hate Stanford? Fast-forward the crisis. A few hours later, Hayden reappears at the Faculty Club where he's been housed. The coordinator is a wreck; Joe-Anne frets not at all.

—I just had a nice long walk. It's quite beautiful here. What's wrong?

2008

What's for Lunch?

(Thom Gunn)

During the years Thom Gunn and I were friends and neighbors, most of our conversation—save the odd chop-chop exchange at our local streetcar stop—was over lunch. Same place (Zazie's, in San Francisco's Cole Valley, midway between our houses), same time (1:00), usually Wednesdays. He could be a rather shy man but had a large manner and charmed waitresses immediately. We talked mostly small talk, sometimes big talk in a careless small talk way, and we laughed. His laughter, pumped by one of his heavy motorcycle boots thumping the floor, contained the raucous completeness of life. The conversation lurched this way and that but always hit writerly gossip, movies, food, books, and sex.

We're quietly picking through and apart poets from across the Bay, and he says of one: "He's a terrible poet, but I don't think he thinks so." Of an article on his work that he feels simply used him to serve the writer's poetic self-interests, he says it's "in bad faith," which reminds me how important existentialism (that now quaint province) was to him, especially the writings of Camus and Sartre, because what really mattered was the *this* and the *now*, living into (not for) the future.

Thom took an almost mischievous delight in announcing his lunch choice. Satisfying appetites of all kinds kept him going strong. We order food and a carafe of white (because it's lunch) wine and swap recipes. He's proud of a "penne with arugula" he cooked for his family this week. In his cooking and eating, as in his poems, he liked bold, candid, straightforward flavors. His enthusiasms burned hot but clean. One thing got textured into something else; culinary taste fused to literary taste. He admired Ben Jonson and Baudelaire because their little-furnace forms—those clocking rhyming meters—could contain fevered appetites and personal anarchy. And yet Thom Gunn was also principled and polite. When I insist one year that I'm treating because it's his birthday ("Happy birthday. And don't be difficult.") he demurs for a moment, casting his eyes down as he did, then allows it, since "it would be ungracious to refuse."

Talking about books was like kvetching about living writers. I mention I'm reading Melville's *Pierre* and he huffs that chesty laugh. The most boring novel ever written! Though he *has*, of course, read it. Another time, it's *The Charterhouse of Parma*, a shared passion, and when I mention how Fabrizio keeps losing his horse in the early chapters, Thom doesn't drop a beat: "He does have a hard time holding his horses, doesn't he?" His favorite episode, though, is Fabrizio's imprisonment. From the chink in his cell's blind he can glimpse the girl he loves only when she comes to her window to feed her birds, which are in cages! Because Thom loved excess and the extremities of eros, he relished the fact that when Fabrizio finally escapes, he turns himself in again because it's the only way he can see Clelia. That found its way into one of his poems.

He knew more about the visual arts than he let on and had faultless taste in choosing cover art for his books. He used his own self-portrait drawing on *The Passages of Joy*. In later life he took special interest in Lucian Freud and kept above his desk a postcard of Freud's painting of himself as an old man, which Thom said reminded him of himself, a picture which eventually occasioned a poem in *Boss Cupid*, whose cover image (by Attila Richard Lucas) of a hipshot skinhead in combat boots, whisked about by a Turner-esque atmosphere, compacted the Ain't-I-a-case, tough-tender sass I liked in his poetry.

Some days we'd spend an entire carafe of white on movies. He loved cop and gangster pictures and was especially keen on nasties like Richard Gere in *Internal Affairs*. He relished the scene where Gere cozies up to a guy who has just caught him sodomizing his wife and who has a gun, which goes off. Gere looks down and, disappointed, says, "Steven, that's my *foot!*" Then he's on to the only impersonation I ever heard him do, of Ben Kingsley in *Sexy Beast*: so revved by the blunt comic force of the word that he can hardly sit still, Thom snarls: "You *cunt!*" He somehow manages to pack inside the epithet an affectionate laugh.

We talked only a little about family, which often got twisted up with the life of poetry. We puzzled over the time and circumstance it takes for experience to settle in the inner life before poets can write it out. The big case for him was "The Gas-Poker," a poem about his mother's suicide over 40 years after the fact. Sometimes he would talk a little about Mike Kitay and the men in his house, and I would talk about my daughter. The time I told him she had just fallen in love—her first great love—with a woman, sweet savvy Thom said: "Now you can both stand on the corner watching all the girls go by."

2005

No Blot, Nor Blank

(Robert Browning)

It's past midnight in Florence's red-light district in the mid-fifteenth century, and a man dressed as a monk has just been strong-armed by the local constabulary and questioned about his presence in such a place. Wait, he says, I can explain everything. That's where we are at the beginning of Browning's "Fra Lippo Lippi." What follows is a wild improvisation on assorted themes—lust, want, religion, art-making, the nature of beauty. The good Fra Lippo *does* explain his presence, explains in fact pretty much his entire life and art, over the course of nearly 400 lines. He is, like other of Browning's monologists, a world-class talker.

Browning wrote many kinds of poetry, but the poems I like best and have been rereading for years are the dramatic monologues, where the ventriloquist poet throws his voice and we hear a dummy (usually an actual historical personage) talk itself into existence. Although the speaker, or talker, is usually directing his carry-on to a particular person or persons, he may as well be talking to himself. The Duke of Ferrara in "My Last Duchess" is in love with the sound of his own voice and cherishes its homicidal menace. A monologue lets the poet shape and set loose a voice that reveals something that matters not just to the speaker but to Browning. The "unknown painter" whose voice we hear in "Pictor Ignotus" is soured by what he feels to be his contemporaries' indifference toward his work. In every monologue we hear the talker (or what I think of as the poems' consciousness) working through a crisis, conducting an argument, or rationalizing inclinations, actions, and beliefs. Some of these poems are about painting and are spoken by artists. Even those not in artists' voices usually involve art. The dying ecclesiast in "The Bishop Orders His Tomb at Saint Praxed's Church," whose thoughts should be concentrated on last things and the afterlife, obsesses about architecture, stonemasonry, and sculpture.

Every Browning monologue cracks open an idiosyncratic, preoccupied mind, and the imaginative arc that connects us to that mind is the same arc we make when reading Shakespeare: it's a character that speaks to us, not the poet, though it's the poet who embodies and gives voice to the character's passions. Browning, like Shakespeare, is everywhere and nowhere in the voices he creates. In "Fra Lippo Lippi," he has his character make a case for Renaissance realism because he wants to make a case for the vivid textures and psychological realism of his own poems, a prime instance of which is the very monologue we're reading. Reading Browning, we're suddenly made eavesdroppers to an already strung-out dramatic situation; it's like hearing one side of a telephone conversation already in progress.

Browning takes nasty delight in dropping us into situations that engage moral questions attached to rough, unpleasant realities, though his tone is high spirited and racy, not morose. "Andrea Del Sarto," spoken by the sixteenth-century artist described by Vasari as "the faultless painter," starts with Del Sarto's attempt to have a relationship talk with his wife: "But do not let us quarrel any more, / No, my Lucrezia; bear with me for once." A few years earlier, Lucrezia persuaded him to return from the Court of France (where he'd been invited and won acclaim and prosperity) to Florence— that is, to her and her claims on him—which he fears may have cost him the supreme fame of a Michelangelo or Raphael. We follow the movements of his mind as it moves through various subjects: good technique, nostalgia, fame, and covetousness. We learn that he's henpecked but loves his wife (in part because she's a reliable model), that he's sensitive to personal and professional slights, and that he's not entirely convinced that being a "perfect painter" is such a good thing after all.

In "My Last Duchess," the greatest modern poem I know about the acidic, murderous dynamics of jealousy, the Duke of Ferrara is showing his art collection to the representative of a nobleman whose daughter the Duke is betrothed to. The collection's centerpiece is a portrait of his lately deceased Duchess, who in life—the Duke lets the go-between (and us) know—distributed her attention to the world too indiscriminately to please the egomaniacal owner "of a nine-hundred-years old name." Was the Duchess superficial and flirty? Did she smile too much at everything alike? We have only the Duke's word for it. There's no ambiguity about the Duke's solution, though: "I gave commands; / Then all smiles stopped together." Listening to him, we're like Othello depending on an Iago for our intelligence.

To read these poems is to experience how idiosyncratic consciousness answers to reality. Whatever the monologist says about the world of circumstance is not a shared truth, it's a person-specific interpretation. Every detail he selects to notice reveals something essential about character. Fra Lippo's improvised self-defense becomes an eloquent, at times hilarious résumé of his orphaned, street-urchin beginnings and how those circumstances shaped his art. This painter so gifted at rendering psychological subtleties in physiognomies was a starving kid who had to recognize which face would bestow on him a crust of bread and which would kick him aside. Want taught him to value the pleasures of the flesh. The deprived child grew to become a less than pious cleric who chases girls. He's one of several priests Browning teased for their randy worldliness. The dying priest in "The Bishop Orders His Tomb" moans reverentially about the blue vein in the Blessed Virgin's breast.

It's not only the "what" of the monologues that wakes us into recognitions of character. The "how" matters just as much. Browning was vilified for obscurity and abused by critics for mangling language. The speed of the thoughts that issue from his speakers' mouths sometimes blurs clarity. But the stream of consciousness is an interrupted, crooked stream, and Browning intentionally lets his speakers indulge in gnarly obliqueness. We have to pay attention to his speakers' patterns of reasoning, however corrupted or manipulative. (Browning's talkers always represent, as we do when we monologue in life, their own interests.) He varies effects poem to poem. "My Last Duchess," a viper of a poem, its beautifully reasoned discourse envenomed with insinuation, is quite unlike the tumbling confusions of the Bishop's last thoughts, which snap back and forth from his envy of another cleric's tomb to his resentment toward his sons (don't ask) to his obsession with lapis lazuli and correct Latin.

The monologues are crafted to reveal the moral character of the speakers, and the crafting depends on the sonorities and rhythms of versification. When Fra Lippo gets serious about the relation of art-making to appetite, his meters turn blunt: "This world's no blot for us, / Nor blank. It means intensely, and means good; / To find its meaning is my meat and drink." But when he describes how, while painting night after night all those saints and Madonnas, his attention was drawn by a sound outside his window, the meters dramatize the excitement and arrested attention he felt when he looked out and saw "Like the skipping of rabbits by moonlight—three slim shapes." The first half of the line prances toward those last three monosyllabic attention stoppers. When he rhymed, he could do so to chilling effect. The rhyming couplets spoken by the smug, righteous Duke in "My Last Duchess" growl with wounded vanity: "She liked whate'er / She looked on, and her looks went everywhere."

Selfhood in Browning is a mass of disheveled fragments of experience, and the monologues give form to what it feels like to actually live them, what it feels like to work at understanding meaning, with little more to go on than memory, desire, and circumstance. He loves to rake life's casual messiness across apparent certitude and aphoristic confidence. "Andrea del Sarto" contains Browning's most famous maxim: "A man's reach should exceed his grasp / Else what's a heaven for." A sparkling nugget, that one. But all around it one hears about the dozens of tiny rips and rents in Andrea's marriage, artistic practice, and worldly career. Readers like myself who savor these poems go to them not for confirmation of what we already know but to experience the lurching, unstable process of making sense of things.

2006

Looking at Pictures

The Jazz Loft

(W. Eugene Smith)

I've been listening to the jazz pianist Dave McKenna, who died in 2008. He was a lyrical swing artist with some of Bill Evans's melancholy, though he wasn't as inventive as Evans and didn't have the emotional range, but at his best his playing had a loping, endearing sweetness. McKenna liked to joke that he wasn't really a jazz stylist, that he was at heart a "saloon piano player." He meant he was a melodist more than an improviser, though in the early 1960s he jammed with some of the greatest improvisers of postwar jazz in a loft building at 861 Sixth Avenue, near 28th Street in Manhattan.

McKenna was a handsome, dashing man back in the day, and we know so because the best snapshot of him was taken in 1960, by W. Eugene Smith, at that Sixth Avenue address. Smith was one of the most famous photographers in America, but in the 1950s his career had taken a hard right. Born in Wichita in 1918, by the 1940s he was working for *Newsweek* and became a combat photographer during WW II; badly wounded in the Pacific theater, he lived with chronic pain (and an addiction to meds) until his death in 1978. In the postwar period his images featured regularly and prominently in *Life* magazine, but in 1955, after years of fiery conflicts with his employer, he quit his *Life* job and, famously obsessive, threw himself into a photo essay on Pittsburgh that started as a three-week assignment that dragged on for four years and remained unfinished. In 1957 he left his wife and four kids

and a fine house in Croton-on-Hudson and moved into the dere-
lict, squalid building on Sixth Avenue to wrap up, he hoped, the
Pittsburgh project. The five-story building was by every report a
rat-hole but was located on what must have been New York's most
fragrant block—the wholesale flower district.

The lofts were being used as jamming and rehearsal rooms
(and, illegally, as crash pads) by musicians who shaped hard bop
and free jazz. Miles, Monk, Don Cherry, Ornette Coleman, Zoot
Sims, Albert Ayler, Jimmy Giuffre, Sonny Rollins, Lee Konitz,
Lee Morgan, and many others, famous and not, would show up
sometime after 11:00 p.m. and play and play and play. Smith was
a cultural omnivore and music one of his favorite foods. From
1957 to 1965, while covering his walls with an expansive mess
of prints from his Pittsburgh project, he photographed musicians
who frequented the joint, photographed, too, from his loft windows, the neighborhood downstairs, its citizens and seasons. He
exposed during those years 1,447 rolls of film and made 40,000
images. He also wired and ran mics through the music rooms,
effectively turning the entire building into a recording studio. His
several reel-to-reel machines picked up, in addition to music and
random conversation, stuff coming over the radio. A tape from
1960 includes: game one of the World Series between the Pirates
and Yankees, Faulkner reading from Light in August, Oral Roberts
healing with hallelujahs. In the end, he filled 1,740 reels with 4,000
hours of material.

Out of this shambling, stunning, hilarious archive came a
terrific traveling exhibition, The Jazz Loft Project, which features
photographs of musicians at play and street views from Smith's
loft. The music pictures aren't high-finish images—they're visual
equivalents of improvisation, pieces of reality found by Smith
while he practiced on his own instrument. A frequent subject is
Hall Overton, one of the most esteemed arrangers of the day and
Monk's collaborator on three performances rehearsed in the loft:
Town Hall in 1959, Lincoln Center in 1963, and Carnegie Hall

in 1964. In one photograph we see Overton in a grubby room seated at one of two pianos: the dilapidated uprights stand side by side, as if waiting for movers. A lonesome hi-hat stands on the floor next to a tape recorder, the two reels rhyming with the twin pianos. A clamp lamp throws dirty light onto a crusty ceiling. The room is like a crummy furnace that produces gold ingots. There was a painter in the building, too, David X. Young, and in one shot of the bassist Jimmy Raney, a trombone lies on the floor like something forgotten, and there are runny paintings on the wall. It's virtually a still life of the tools and inchoate forms from which shapely feeling emerges. Smith caught the tremulous acuity of light as it struck surfaces like the lacquer on that trombone, the brass of that hi-hat.

The most compelling images in the show, however, are the ones Smith took from his loft studio. He assumed formal constraints. His windows were viewfinders within his viewfinder. Virtually all the pictures look down to or across Sixth Avenue. He sometimes used a broken windowpane as a framing device, so that certain street scenes look carved up. All the pictures are literally eavesdroppings. We're watching people who don't know they're being watched. Smith was an extremely difficult, self-absorbed person, but his pictures teem with generosity and inclusiveness for the otherness of strangers. A man bundled against an April snowstorm holds a bag of flowers that look like brave beacons of springtime. A woman's leg stepping from a car is a *Mad Men* slice of time without that show's annoying, meticulous perfectionism: Smith delivers the slurred completeness of a lived (and witnessed) moment, and it's a thrill. And when you overhear snippets from the tapes, because there's no sophisticated isolating and tracking of the voicings of instruments and their musicians, you feel like you're in a crowd. It sounds like life.

Flower shops, Sam's Luncheonette, an auto accident (and its victim), cop cars, the delicate spinning-top dance of umbrellas, parade goers carrying little flags, an earnest fellow looking through a telescope after dark—these were Smith's unknowing subjects. Because of his vantage, the weather in the photos often looks laid on, not something blowing or falling through a scene. In his several pictures of plump falling snow, the photographic paper looks flocked and deckled, as if the snow had somehow saturated it. Like most street photographers, Smith was mad for signage. The posted cigarette ads he caught on film seem a nearly forgotten dialect: Chesterfield, L&M, Parliament, Spud. (Spud escapes me.) And that picture I mentioned of flowers in the snow (*First Day of Spring*) contains also a one-way sign pointing in the direction opposite the flowers.

Many of the musicians at Sixth Avenue dropped from sight, some turning up years later in small combos in resorts, others in very different lives. The bassist Jimmy Stevenson, who appears in several Smith pictures, left New York in the 1960s and vanished. In 1998 the writer Sam Stephenson began archiving, editing, and selecting the recorded and photographic material Smith left. When he went in search of musicians who had been part of the loft scene, he eventually found Stevenson in 2003, who with his wife was selling homemade wind chimes at a roadside stand in California wine country. Smith's photographs tell us over and over that life is change and movement. The world below his window was a world at work and in motion. Firefighters, shoppers, laborers lifting man-hole covers, a guy rolling two folded mattresses down the street, delivery trucks, children with their families, mounted police on patrol—so much *direction*! A pair of photos shows a Smurf-y guy in a T-shirt trying to cross Sixth Avenue. He turns this way, then that way, his body torqued as if the city's energy were spinning and confusing him. My favorite image in the exhibition is also the classic representation of all the stories musical and streetside that Smith documented. From the loft window we look down on a woman under a dainty umbrella, a fixed sweet spot in a scene surrounded by busy foot tracks going every which way in slushy snow. The umbrella looks like it has paused for the moment, just before the walker left behind tracks of her own.

2012

The Writing on the Wall

(The Graffiti-ists)

A Medusa recently appeared in my neighborhood. I live in San Francisco, three blocks from Haight Street. I don't go down there much; it's sordid with out-of-towners, shoe stores, homeless folk, and all-purpose muckiness. I feel knocked about by the consumerism and other kinds of greasy neediness on display. That said, there's a thing of beauty on the Masonic Street wall that serves as gateway to the Haight, a mural by the tattoo artist, LANGO: his Medusa parts her lips in an ecstasy of power and allure, a mass of toothy serpents squirming fatly around her head, flirting with their mistress (and us). It seethes with svelte, baleful energy. LANGO's Medusa, like his other murals around the city, is madly compelling in a street-language way. Some say this isn't fine art, but he and other good draftsmen-tattooists follow, in their hyperbolic way, Paul Klee's advice to artists: "Take a line for a walk."

The graffiti tradition tracks back to prehistoric petroglyphs and cave paintings, though those practices were bonded to belief systems or sacred rituals. Contemporary graffiti culture—street artists call it writing, tagging, or bombing—started in late 1960s Philadelphia when a kid named CORNBREAD spray-canned his name and a crown on his reform school's wall, on an elephant in the zoo, and on the Jackson 5's private jet. His strikes became public record of the impulses behind street art that swarmed cities in the 1970s and 1980s: anti-institutionalism and an anti-authority, anti-advertising animus that aspired to advertise an authority of its own. CORNBREAD pioneered the urge to let no blank public space go unheeded.

Art in the Streets, an exhibition that filled the cavernous Geffen Contemporary in Los Angeles' Little Tokyo, isn't only about graffiti or street art. It's a carpet-bomb exhibition that covers as explosively as possible not just the art itself—some of these taggers are very good artists—but all the culture streams that have flowed into or provided inspiration or infrastructure for street art. The confluence includes: outlaw taggers who broke into New York rail yards and turned the sides of subway cars into mural surfaces awash with thrashing, zipper-y, comic imagery; the Lower East Side gallery scene that tried to commercialize street art without taming or domesticating it; L.A.'s *cholo* culture, its lowrider car art, gang life, and tattoos; skateboarding, with its hang-dog costuming and daring public-performance acrobatics; and *its* cultural precedent, breakdancing. Tumble these cultural dust storms with the music of the times—the Sex Pistols, the Clash, the Tom Tom Club, Los Van Van—and you'll approach, but only approach, the experiential overload of *Art in the Streets*.

Subway writers' blocky, jagged, melting forms boast the daring of image-making-as-perilous-act. We can only sense and appreciate this remotely, however, because most of the items on view are, obviously, photographs of the cars and walls that showcased bombers' art. If you actually rode the New York subway back in the day you'll find that the photographs scrub the imagery of its fuzzy city-grime surround, but, stacked like motley Lego tiles, they convey the rolling-carnival spirit of the enterprise. They pump up and primp the colors, too, so that the streaming "walls" have a more vibratory look than they actually did, but the photos are true to certain effects—the atomized color fields, the zoomy elasticity, and the Necco Wafer palette. The exhibition samples street art's stylistic variety: Kenny Scharf's mildly deranged, cutesy-poo, darkly comic fantasies; FUTURA's fervid Kandinsky-esque pops and flashes; Lee Quiñones' ferocious street politics; and the delicate, sweet-natured drawings Keith Haring chalked on blank black subway advertisement panels. The best of the work fused urban jitters with Magical Mystery Tour charm.

The graffiti that actually infested New York subway interiors didn't charm. Jeffrey Deitch, organizer of the exhibition, writes in the catalog that in the mid-1970s, "the New York subways were like total works of art." That's a partisan view. Total works of art they may have been, but that's not to say the art was good. Besides, subway riders didn't get the opportunity to choose the art that was imposed on them and that, inside the cars, invaded their psychological privacies. The random scrawls and slashing incoherent imagery were like obnoxiously loud fellow riders ranting unintelligibly about subjects that had nothing to do with your life. See the 1982 photo of LADY PINK seated against the background of one of her early scrambled tags. Call me unhip, but that kind of anonymous hostile visual noise made a lot of people nervous (as if New Yorkers need worse nerves) and put a chokehold of fear and random anger on a shared, relatively civil public space.

As for the hip and the unhip, *Art in the Streets* plays a shady gambit with those who have misgivings about street art and perform their own derring-do by criticizing it: the conscience behind the show seizes the higher ground of imperturbable, cool knowingness. If you don't dig, you ain't hip. Or you're among the culture elite that taggers tweaked and teased. This sort of curatorial sandbagging co-opts criticism. (The show's subtitle should be that tart bit of street talk: "It's all good.") I detest this kind of let's-get-down high-handedness that thinks it knows what really matters much better than we do. It's cynical elitism of a special, dressed-down kind, and it smacks of condescension to the very artists it claims to value. To this poorly educated white boy raised on the streets of South Philadelphia, part of a museum's mission is to encourage the exercise and sharpening of one's discriminative intelligence.

If I want to be bullied by haranguing visuals and sounds, as I do in fact sometimes want to be, I'll go see *Inception* or Lady Gaga.

I don't mean to tar the artists with that brush. Some of the work is good, really good. My favorites are Richard Hambleton's streaked black human figures that drain starkly down walls or stride like raggedy shadows in a hurry to get nowhere. He splashed many from his "Shadowman" series in places where passersby would suddenly come upon them. They're as streetwise as it gets, they're formally exciting, and they mess with your psyche. Street art, though, like any other, is susceptible to mannerism. Once three-dimensional drop shadows were developed, they quickly became a limp default mode, and the cultivated visual velocity (subway painting looks broomed sidewise by wind) and congestive, obsessively repetitive forms got stale, too.

To judge by the reactions of visitors the day I was there, *Art in the Streets* is a great show for kids and their families, maybe because they don't even try to process the experience, or maybe they perceptually handle a lot more input than I can. I've never felt so pounded and depleted, and I'm someone who values energy for its own sake—in art, music, club life, whatever—but all mere energy all the time makes for jangling boredom, and *Art in the Streets* is that kind of experience. I kept yearning for the sort of contemplative pause that some of the work on display occasions. Banksy's sooty, vaguely melancholy wall figures—a brass band, a child clutching a TV, a baby pouting in her galvanized-pail bathtub—are visitors from other realities taking up residence in ours. Stelios Faitakis' mural, a complex narrative that engages Byzantine art, street uprisings, urban architecture, and sex, has an exquisite, brazen finish. And the writing Jean-Michel Basquiat did when he was still SAMO (before his paintings started making millions for him and his handlers) scratched out urban telegrams composed by a gently naughty but also truly vexed streetside seer. Too much of the stuff on view, though, clamors for our attention like needy children. Good art wakes us into a freshly reimagined experience of familiar realities. Most street art wakes us by yelling at us. Then again, if the exhibition weren't so audacious, I never would have seen an enchanting and absolutely nutty object: in a room featuring a mural-ed lowrider stood an enameled tangerine-flake baby stroller, which for an instant made me wish I'd had a different sort of childhood.

2011

Renoir's Girls

By the 1880s Renoir was well established and well-to-do. He'd already fought what he called *les combats de l'impressionnisme* and triumphed as the impressionist with the most glamorous palette, the sunniest disposition, and the most festive eye for the passages of ordinary life that he, Degas, Manet, and Caillebotte all savored. Unlike them, he was a constant connoisseur of happiness. His 1881 *Luncheon of the Boating Party*—riverside table tipsy with wine, food and flowers; revelers bridging social classes, from swells in top hats and frock coats to rivermen in straw stingy-brims and T-shirts; lively flirtations (including one between a redhead and her lapdog) slouching throughout the scene—has become a poster image for *la belle époque* that would crash during Renoir's lifetime with the outbreak of The Great War.

During the 1880s he got impatient with Impressionism's fleet "touch" and its tousled, snatched-from-life effects. Like most artists, Renoir comes out of predecessors, and to refresh himself after "Impressionism's wars" he looked back to the staginess of eighteenth-century French painting and to Boucher in particular. One would think Renoir had already gotten as rosy as it gets without adding Boucher's flouncy pastoral and boudoir beatitudes, but in Boucher's azure zephyrs and peaches-and-cream complexions Renoir saw a stolid contentment he aspired to. By the 1890s, his passion for Rubens and for the classical modeling and sumptuous interiors of the Veronese and Titian in particular was helping Renoir achieve a riper representation of the female form and a more compact theatricality of interior spaces.

Toward the end of the century, he made two major moves. Advised by doctors in 1897 to seek a warmer climate for his increasingly debilitating rheumatoid arthritis, he moved to Cagnes-sur-Mer in the south of France. He also pretty much gave up painting *en plein air* and moved indoors to create what he called "the outdoors in the studio." Most pictures from this period are interiors that showcase females: children, adolescents, and adults, nude and clothed, performing domestic tasks like sewing or tending children or sharing parlor pastimes like reading and music-making. Renoir's friend and intellectual companion, the Symbolist poet Stéphane Mallarmé, so admired the 1892 *Young Girls at the Piano*—the girls' languid concentration blends into their creamy physiques—that he persuaded the French government to acquire it. Renoir in turn was interested in Mallarmé's poetics, which preferred evocation to denotation, obliquity to directness, rhapsodic illusion to hard reality, and he translated Symbolist poetry's mercurial syntax, its mystery-flow, into swooning pictorial reverie.

The later paintings beam and beckon, and they're lightheaded with Renoir's enthusiasm for his motifs. This isn't the same as being lightheaded about his models. ("It's the painter who makes the model," he said.) Rilke wrote in 1906 that certain artists, Cézanne most of all, drain personal affection from their work. A Cézanne picture doesn't say, "I love this;" it says, "Here it is." Cézanne leaves the love out. Renoir leaves it in, leaves in a love for his self-induced vision of the feminine. If you're slain with pleasure by the corpulent big-hipped torsos, petite heads, and brightly flushed cheeks of women in Renoir's late work, the exhibition *Renoir in the Twentieth Century*, which tracks Renoir's practice from 1890 up to his death in 1919, will fill you up. If you have misgivings about the look of the feminine in Renoir's later work, stay with me and allow me a digression.

Personal taste is irrational, visceral, appetitive, always a little mysterious. Mostly, though, taste is judgment. As a young man taking in the suave, shimmying color of Renoir's later work—some of his choicest things are in my hometown, in the Philadelphia Museum of Art and the Barnes—to me his women pictures, the nudes in particular, were astonishments with a hubba-hubba element. Over the years, as I've revisited his work and soaked up the art of his contemporaries, my feeling for the work changed, and in the exhibition those same Philadelphia pictures look redundant, mannered, self-pleasuring. Renoir's fields of flesh now look like massive drapery, a décor, and the pert girlie heads mounted on stout, mature, Titian-esque bodies look sweetly grotesque.

The exhibition includes work by contemporaries who admired and learned from Renoir. In the room containing two Renoir pictures of nudes bathing—his sinuous color-streams rush and roil from long swept-back hair into background fog and bath sheets wetly pasted to skin—my eye kept being snapped away from them to a 1912 Bonnard, *Woman at Her Window*. Bonnard's wife's lean figure fills half the frame; a slash of vermillion peignoir droops from her vanity. She stands, legs apart, looking out the window, turned away indifferently from the painter's gaze. She's not being adoringly served up to us. The picture doesn't announce a painterly program. It enacts the struggle to still the movements of the artist's inner life (as it reflects not only on the feminine but on reality and the forms that mediate and load with passion the zone between feeling and reality) in the stilled movements of line and color. Bonnard isn't enshrining the feminine for pious male ardor, he's prying into and dismantling Renoir's nouveau classical ideals. Renoir's bathers say, "Look at us." Bonnard's picture says, "Watch me." *Woman at Her Window* teaches us to see carnality afresh, moving our eye from one unpredictable passage to another as if to remind us that the feminine isn't a totem, it's a delicately tentative work in progress. Bonnard's hand teases out a provisional vision. Renoir's is taking dictation from a mail-order Aphrodite. Stretched, faintly marbled rotundities of flesh monumentalize virtually every female image Renoir made after 1890. That's exactly what he intended. I don't question the flamboyant execution and beauty-on-demand effect. I question his vision of the feminine.

Some of the last pictures are Renoir's finest. Whatever one's misgivings, a few of the nudes achieve a pastel ethereality and veiledness that make those bulky bodies look afloat in bower or bed. And he made other sorts of pictures. The 1905 landscape, *Terrace at Cagnes*, bristles with an exploratory feverishness: bushy clusters and twiggy trees surround a small red figure sitting on a terrace; behind her, hillside houses shove each other high in the picture towards a sliding blue sky. And in the more naturalistic work—a society couple, a young man hunting, a youth in Pierrot costume—the compositional weave of setting and garments and skin shakes looser than ever. *Terrace at Cagnes*'s bright palette recalls Impressionism's salad days, but in Renoir's best late pictures old age brought a restorative darkening, as a great singing voice darkens with age, especially in his rendering of women playing instruments, which twenty years earlier had been his coziest subject. With the more shadowed tonality, the pictures gain an animated reflectiveness, a small nervousness of mind that give them a mildly quaking intensity we don't associate with Renoir. He liked to say that painting was "made to beautify," and in the soberly gorgeous *The Concert*, one of his last pictures, whirlpooling textures sweep and tumble together roses, wallpaper, mandolin, hair scarves, liquid gowns, and necklines that look like gulf shores defining the women's dreamy topographies. It invites us to lose ourselves. Life and aging brought Renoir a hard march of physical suffering— there are films of him painting with a brush tied to his crippled arthritic hand—but he was a poet of joy to the end, and even if we don't share the joy or admire its style of representation, we have to recognize that that's what it is.

2010

Varnishing Days

(J. M. W. Turner)

Painters in mid-nineteenth-century London, when installing exhi-
bitions at official venues like the Royal Academy of Arts and the
British Institution, brought not quite finished pictures to what
were called Varnishing Days, where they discussed each other's
work and applied a finish to their pictures. J. M. W. Turner, especially in his later years, pushed the purpose of Varnishing Days
to the extreme. He often brought work still in the early stages of
completion then elaborated details, shaping narrative content and
working up his most signature mercurial effects. Turner never
lacked a sense of self-drama, and these virtuoso displays, part mis-
chief but mostly the natural consequence of the nervous energy he
poured into his work, became notorious events. By age 60, though
esteemed and well off, he was more than ever an object of contempt
by journalists and connoisseurs. It looked as if the excitableness
that had characterized his pictures for so long was becoming his
real subject. The contested, explosive work of his late years, from
the 1830s to his death in 1851, is the subject of *J. M. W. Turner:
Painting Set Free*.

Joseph Mallord William Turner was born in London in 1775.
His father, a barber and wig-maker, recognized his son's gifts early
and by age fourteen Turner was attending the Royal Academy,
where he would later teach. He was an extremely ambitious young
artist determined to establish a major reputation. Landscapes, great
houses, marine pictures, treatments of historical subjects and con-

temporary events—Turner wanted it all. Around 1818 he'd made a series of paintings about the rise and fall of ancient Carthage *and* a grim picture of the carnage on the battlefield of Waterloo. He was also a documentarian of industrialized modernity, especially its steamships and railways. He expressed the newness of the age with an incendiary stylistic newness.

In the 1830s Turner's work became looser, more diffuse and volatilized, and his critics became more rabid, comparing his work to soapsuds, whitewash, mustard. One caricaturist depicted him at his easel wielding a mop, with a pail of yellow paint at his feet. It was obvious by the 1830s that every picture was in some way an occasion for challenging his materials. The execution was loaded with emotion: Turner painted his feeling for depicted events by generating fierce atmospherics created to surround or emanate from such events. You recognize a late Turner before recognizing its anecdotal content. Blizzards, rainstorms, biblical winds—any prodigious force of nature brought forth a response that, in the language of the canvas, aspired to meet force with force. The radiance in the pictures seems almost hysterical and the restless darkness as unforgiving and devouring as any painter has given us.

Consider *The Burning of the Houses of Lords and Commons, 16 October 1834*. The fire started at night and drew a large crowd, Turner among them. It was exhibited at the British Institution, and another artist said that Turner brought to Varnishing Days a canvas that had just barely a primary lay-in of color and did the pyrotechnical detail work there. He created a contagion of combustion: Westminster Bridge seems to catch fire and melt into the flames that whip from the Houses. It's an of-the-moment event but, like other Turner pictures, folds into contemporary event something anachronistic, something "other." While *The Burning* swarms with the torchlight the fire creates, in the dark foreground a group of women talks to someone dressed in medieval clerical garb. These "outsiders" have their backs to the fire, as if watching the watchers, a ceremonial past observing a contemporary chaos.

The steamship, introduced in the 1810s, transformed the shipping industries, and by the 1830s it was one of Turner's subjects, but the mechanization steamships represented didn't distract him from the sublime, which became the cosmic envelope that raveled up technology. He came of age when the Romantic poets were at their peak powers. Keats died in 1821, Shelley, 1822, Wordsworth, 1850, and Turner was as concerned with the nature of nature as the poets were. (He was literary and left behind an unfinished historical epic, *Fallacies of Hope*.) His earlier paintings had a histrionic grandeur, but from the 1830s on, nature became an even more agitated theater of impartial and indifferent force, of cones and gyres and spikes of light and rain and darkness. His 1842 *Snow Storm* makes me think of mad Lear on the heath: "Blow, winds, and crack your cheeks! Rage! Blow! / You cataracts and hurricanoes . . ." We see a steamboat trapped and tossed in a whirlwind, its hull indistinguishable from the rotund upswelling of the sea: grand circulatory vortices of grays, blacks, and browns scoop up and around the vessel while it shoots off phosphorescent signaling rockets.

When treating historical or classical subjects, Turner liked to shrink anecdotal content, as if to check the relative scale of human event against nature's process. He deposits the action of *Regulus* (about a self-sacrificing Roman general who turns himself over to his Carthaginian enemies, who imprison him then cut off his eyelids and expose him to the sun) in the picture's lower left pocket, a vague concentrate of action. What overwhelms the viewer is a sulfurous hourglass of yellow-white light that spools down through the picture. You feel Turner aspiring to a pictorial language equivalent to the expressive energies nature possessed. His most sensuous effects are often the most vaporous. His contemporary Constable said his pictures were "painted with tinted steam."

To his students, Turner's advice about watercolors was: "First of all, respect your paper!" He made watercolors wet on wet, putting color into not-yet-dry color, and he used already wet paper sometimes treated with animal glue, which made the paper less absorbent. The colors, for all the speediness of application, sometimes have a congealed, mounded profile, as if *gathered* into form. His watercolors of Venice in particular possess (and induce) the astonishment of his oil paintings, but the medium gives them more quivery dynamics, apt for a city so heavily inflected by the lagoon that contains it. In *Fishermen on the Lagoon, Moonlight*, moonlight whitens the sky then shafts down through the water's surface and breaks up to create an underbed of luminosity. The fishermen on their platform and boats are fragile materializations of darkness within the enveloping nocturnal light.

There's an extreme yet celebratory urgency in many of Turner's pictures, and a visionary purpose. He folds into an of the instant natural event both its fore-moment and premonitions of its after-moment. He was a poet of colossal circumstantiality. His surfaces' fabulous, uneven topographies document his spontaneous process and emotional intensity. In any marine painting you're likely to find a jet or surge of surf rendered as an archipelago of lumps and blots of pigment, and the streaky layering can look like yellowing scar tissue, *beautiful* scar tissue: it's as if he's in a compulsive rush to register one effect so that he can chase yet another.

Turner's pictures of the whaling industry are among the most exciting things in *Painting Set Free*. He creates a busy field of contesting teeming masses, of sun and sea beating against the whalers' activities—the harpooning, the hoisting of a whale's head, the rendering of blubber. But the exhibition also provides a lot of evidence for Turner's control over a variety of emotional tones. When the familiar incandescent energy gets sober and subdued, you feel a turbulent world has been momentarily becalmed. In pastoral pictures from his several Italian excursions, when a tree appears it becomes a strong axial compass for the stirring airs surrounding it. The tree looks steadfast and enduring.

2015

Rembrandt All Over

In the late 1640s and 1650s, the Netherlands' prosperous Golden Age dimmed. Hundreds of businesses failed, and a major recession enfeebled the entire society. Even Rembrandt, renowned and rich, hit a wall, partly of his own construction. He'd bought the equivalent of a tycoon's mansion beyond his means, spent lavishly to acquire an art collection he really couldn't afford, and expected the art market to continue to reward his tireless genius. Instead, his many tuition-paying students flooded the market with work that competed with their master's, his client list shrunk, he defaulted on his mortgage, and by 1656 he was bankrupt. The handsome inheritance he might have received when his beloved wife Saskia died in 1642 was contingent on his not remarrying, and when he did take up with another love, Hendricke Stoffels, she (and by implication her nonhusband) was publically chastised by Calvinist elders for her loose ways. *And* Rembrandt's painterly manner, so dominant for so long, was quietly falling from favor.

During these bad times he still produced great work, in particular a series I saw recently in San Diego of etchings on New Testament subjects. Rembrandt had market incentive: prints were quicker and easier to make and sell than paintings. The "Gospel" etchings are a canny equivalent for our own lean times. The fifteen prints are elegantly installed, with generous meditative spacing between them, on pale gray walls that kick up the prints' dark radiance. You don't feel hurried and aren't badgered by earnest, tendentious wall labels, and each work is a busy country of meaning. The old masters chose religious subjects (as certain young masters still do) because they're fraught with action, character, conflict of all kinds, and because they ignite urgent passions. When scriptural events or personalities elicit feelings specific to the artist's own life experience—Fra Angelico's piety, Lippo Lippi's worldliness, Caravaggio's carnal voracity—the work carries a *Boom!* charge. Rembrandt's Shakespearean curiosity, about human nature, transformation, inwardness evidenced by physical expressiveness, and the demons fate sends our way, is played out in his paintings. The etchings are compelling because he was forcing another, more stringent medium (scores and scrapes on copper plate) to yield more physically expansive, pictorially complex imagery than his predecessors had done. Rembrandt gets you lost in the wiry surges and mass-attack actions of line, and in his scenes from the life of Jesus you feel that personal emotional compulsion is pitching his imagination to existential extremes.

In *Christ Preaching*, the Messiah is a saddened, fatigued street-corner preacher, and the crowd Rembrandt assembles around him is a mildly tranquilized Shakespearean rabble: a few bored, hungry faces; a kid fooling around in the dirt, indifferent to the news-bringer; and an old woman so distracted by her own misery that she looks slightly deranged. Above Christ's head hovers a puny oval halo, drizzled with light. And Rembrandt's black lines create such light! In a crucifixion scene, thicketed cross-hatchings and curvilinear swells create a storm of confusion, fury, catastrophe—the celestial light that drains down looks like a tightly strung instrument, the entire scene a heaven-and-earth sound box.

Etching calls attention to the mechanics of scene engineering. In *The Descent from the Cross by Torchlight*, Rembrandt reduces Christ to an animal mass difficult to maneuver because of its dead weight. His head and dangling arm are sorrow-heavy. It reminded me of the strength and care required of Joseph of Arimathea and

Nicodemus to get the body down from the cross without further mutilating it, and that the come-and-go torchlight made the removal all the more precarious. In *Christ Presented to the People (Ecce Homo)*, Rembrandt makes Christ nearly a shrunken wretch next to the self-important Pilate. He organizes the stage action—or, rather, inaction, since the surrounding onlookers look so impassive—around the civic-center porch they stand on. His staging suggests a sacrificial altar, a dry run Golgotha tricked out as a kind of City Hall appearance. Rembrandt was depositing all kinds of personal anger and grief into works like *Ecce Homo*, but there's also an ethereal tenderness in, of all things, *Christ on the Mount of Olives (The Agony in the Garden)*, in which the angel's wing, raised like an accusing hand above the disciples sleeping in the background, is also cocked to protect the desolate Jesus but won't, can't really, shield him from the ominous soldiers sketchily visible behind the wing.

The Rembrandt etchings were displayed along with prints by his most gifted student, Ferdinand Bol, born in 1616 and one of many assistants who worked in the master's studio. Bol did that for about six years then established his own practice as a painter. He produced only twenty-two known etchings, but they so boldly flashed the technical finesse he learned from Rembrandt (who, unstoppable as usual, made over three hundred) that his work was sometimes mistaken for his teacher's. On a few prints you can see where light-fingered dealers scratched Rembrandt's name in place of Bol's. Rembrandt was Rembrandt, but there's enough of Bol's work to impress us with his gifts and outline the dynamics of borrowing and imitation that churned between master and student. One rarity, the only known impression of Bol's *Saskia with Pearls in Her Hair*, adapts Rembrandt's 1634 etching of the same title, and since it's unsigned the attribution is still a little shaky, but the floating ringlets and curlicues are signs of Bol's later style, though it's a style closely tied to Rembrandt's. Bol built on the master's techniques to develop his own oscillating effects in fabrics, and mid-1600s Netherlandish art revered rich stuffs and exotic costumes. All painters made "tronies," portraits of subjects dressed in fictive, historical dress, the more opulent the better—Rembrandt's studio must have looked like a wardrobe trailer on a film set—and they fancied scenes of substantial women leaning out windows or half doors. My favorite Rembrandt used to be an Art Institute painting of Saskia looking out a Dutch door, until experts determined that Rembrandt didn't paint it. It's still one of my favorites pictures, but my favorite Rembrandt it can no longer be. Bol made a sensuous etching of a woman leaning out a window offering passersby (i.e., us) a pear and her come-up-and-see-me-sometime allure. The pear's curves repeat the U-shaped necklace dangling above a scooped-neck dress.

Bol learned much from Rembrandt's way of cross-hatching tonal zones and mass. Rembrandt's work, though, is more finely modulated passage to passage, from cavernous shadow to the wiry delicacy of beads, women's hair, and textiles. And the gift of representing human character can't be learned. You either have a feeling for it or you don't. Bol didn't quite have Rembrandt's way with eyes as repositories and instruments of feeling. In his best etchings, the eyes seem to look inward even as they look out on the world. In *Self-portrait with Saskia* Rembrandt depicts himself in a dashing feathered hat: he's a world-beater, full of beans, more than a little arrogant. Saskia stands behind his shoulder, demure, calmly self-contained, but her look is custodial: her man may be the player, but she's the stakeholder.

Rembrandt was the more audacious, but he and Bol both pushed etching toward finer textural expressiveness and subtler lighting. The buoyant angel in Bol's *Gideon's Sacrifice* floats upon the earth dressed not so much in a seraphic gown as in a sketchily outlined phantasmal *whiteness*. And the dry-point lines and cross-hatching in Rembrandt's *St. Jerome in a Dark Chamber* strain bright window light through tattered curtains toward a wall's scoured surface that gradually darkens to nearly monotonal darkness: in the middle zone sits Jerome, his mediating human intelligence operating in the middle passage between vague light and storm-cloud darkness. The closer you scrutinize these things, the more lost you become in the tumbling of line and mass. Their energy feels like a desirable contagion.

2010

Sacred Space

(Giovanni Bellini)

Pictures sometimes become devotional objects or pilgrimage destinations. Their contents have the feeling of secular-sacred spaces. The room called the Living Hall in New York's Frick Collection houses several robust portraits, Titian's force-of-nature *Portrait of Pietro Aretino* among them. But the image visitors get stuck on is Giovanni Bellini's *St. Francis in the Desert*. I know New Yorkers (and out-of-towners like me) who go to the Frick to stand with practiced reverence before it. Emerging from his wilderness hermitage, Francis steps into the light with outspread arms (posed, some think, to receive the stigmata) and from the lower right corner where he stands a sleek spatial energy bells up and outward to encompass rocky landscape, animals, a Bellini-blue sky (a cerulean violet-green), and in the distance a city, the culture of civilization that heroic, pious solitaries aspire to saturate and shape. It's the kind of expressiveness you want to inhale into your life-spirit, if you believe in such a state. Bellini's Francis and his expansive scene can leave you flush with praise, psalmic praise, a grand tumble of awe, unreason, and joy.

What is a secular-sacred site? Many visitors to the Rothko Chapel in Houston, designed to be a nondenominational meditative space, find it a spare, quiet, but not churchy place crafted to encourage one to confront one's being, in the moment, in the world, in whatever atomic scheme of things one believes in, watched over by the dark Druidic presences of Rothko's pictures. In traditional Christian iconography, wastes and barrens and gardens become holy stations where transcendent events transpire: a hermitage, a road to Damascus, a wedding hall. But in our secular lives nearly any place can become such a zone: a soup kitchen; a luxe living room; a subway car or café; riverside, wood, hilltop—fraught hollows where we may consider the world and *its* consciousness. Time alters. A moment, once we're in our contemplative head and heart, becomes a mysteriously stretched zone of vision, maybe exaltation. We don't want it to end and in that moment of resistance we also know it must.

I'm thinking on these matters because of an exhibition at the Getty Center, *Giovanni Bellini: Landscapes of Faith in Renaissance Venice*. In the decades leading to the extreme eruption of genius (Titian, Tintoretto, Veronese) in sixteenth-century Venetian painting, Bellini was the most sought after painter of small-sized devotional pictures. Well-to-do patrons, of which there were an increasing number in Venice's world-dominating maritime economy, commissioned private images—a Crucifixion, a Madonna and Child, a *sacra conversazione* convening three or more holy presences, a Jerome in the wilderness, a Francis in his hermitage—to serve as contemplative objects and occasions for prayer, which may be simply an act of extreme attention, or a self-preparedness for an (unanticipated) answer from Deity, or, as the poet George Herbert wrote, simply "something understood." To consider a garden or landscape in a Bellini picture was to consider the various expressions of virginity, chastity, purity, and divine order, not just in the natural world but in any disordered or beseeching heart seeking respite, clarity, harmony.

Bellini was born in 1435 and came of age training and working with his famous father, Jacopo, when influences from Florentine painting and its passion for draughtsman-like clarity of structure and color were being met by the northern influence of artists like Dürer and their insistent naturalism, especially in their representations of nature. Bellini was also born into a world of one sort of artistic practice and left the world (in 1516) in another. For many years he worked in the medium of quick-drying egg tempera on a wooden support. After the introduction in Italy of slow-drying oil paints from the North, like other painters he took advantage of oils' colorist pliancy. As the century wore on, paintings destined for exercises of piety turned more to the epic, sumptuary, public narratives that were already filling Venice's churches and confraternities. Bellini would paint these, too, grandly paint them, as witness his altarpieces in San Zaccaria and the Frari.

Bellini's holy figures possess an ineffable tenderness and interiority. His Saint Dominic lives deeply inside himself, as if in constant review of a tested, vigilant inner life. He's pictured reading a large book with such attentiveness and contentment that he dramatizes the deepest spiritual pleasures of the act of reading. And in *Virgin and Child with Saint John the Baptist and a Female Saint in a Landscape*, Mary looks down on the infant in her lap with a resigned heaviness that tells us she knows she's sadly prepared to surrender her child for sacrifice. Her context is the rest of the world: the landscape behind her is composed of city, sea, ship, fields, shepherds, which don't just provide a worldly topography of creation but a directory of life functions, of commerce, fertility, provisioning, sponsorship, and overseeing.

In Bellini's crucifixion scenes, we see him picture to picture experimenting with the dilating or contracting of space. Every degree calculates an emotional effect. In one scene Christ isn't embedded in a quotidian natural environment or made one more object in nature's landscapes, he's instead offered up in his agonized solitude on the rocky sacrificial altar of Golgotha. He looks abandoned and, as his sweaty face and bloody head testify, drained of hope. It's a terrible image of lostness. In *Crucifixion With the Virgin and Saint John the Evangelist*, Bellini's interest doesn't lie so much in sacred story as in the streaming of life behind the Passion event. It's an essay on the relation of sacred story to the physical reality of the natural order, which reminds us of Christ as an event in history, an action among us, not a mere object of veneration. Bellini's globalizing vision pulls it all together in one scene in consciousness. The freshness of his landscapes enacts fresh beginnings.

Landscape, with its plain fresh beauties and symbolic resonance, figures in the Getty's companion exhibition, *Sacred Landscapes: Nature in Renaissance Manuscripts*, an intense, compact tour of book illustrations from France, Italy, and the Netherlands more or less contemporaneous with Bellini's career. Wealthy patrons commissioned Books of Hours, illustrated prayer books wherein a needy or troubled mind might find shelter, direction, solace. The exhibition includes imagery from one made for a young woman named Denise Poncher. An illustration shows her kneeling, prayer book in hand, before an extremely tall, worm-infested, skin-raggedy skeleton bestriding three recent victims. It's a terrifying picture and reminds us how *not* far we've come, in the popular imagination at least, from our envisioning of death, who is grinning and wielding several scythes: one blade curls around the kneeling Denise's head like a dreadful lure that would swipe her away from the lush life-burst of vegetation around her. In another *Noli mi tangere*, she's met by the risen Christ, bloody but dressed in crown and robes of a gold that threads through the pious girl's tresses and spangles the natural world in which both figures are set. Everything looks touched and shockingly changed by the Redeemer's bloody sacrifice.

I have two pocket-sized favorites in *Sacred Landscapes*. A tiny (5" x 3") cutting of the letter "S," from a gradual attributed to Pisanello dated 1440-1450, dramatizes the conversion of St. Paul. In the image's upper hemisphere an opulently attired noble in an imperial red turban and livery rides confidently with two soldiers; in the lower hemisphere, in the lower crook of the "S," an armored Paul tumbles gracelessly, helplessly, from his horse. And in a creation scene from a prayer book, in a field of lilies, irises, roses, and an intensely green scaly date palm, Eve's body rises from Adam's rib, one leg still half-sunken in his torso. She's *stepping out!* In the background we see them as it were a minute later, the two reaching for forbidden fruit, then a little deeper in the small scene they're being expelled from the garden, and highest in the scene are their sons offering sacrifice. These, too, are beginnings—inauspicious ones.

2017

Picture Perfect

(Ruud van Empel)

The Garden of Eden is a foundational dream in consciousness. It's where (in the Jerusalem Bible's version of Genesis) "Yahweh caused to grow every kind of tree, enticing to look at and good to eat," and Yahweh settled man in the garden of Eden "to cultivate and take care of it." When the woman and man ate fruit of the Tree of the Knowledge of Good and Evil, that sweet thing inducted the couple into an existence of pain and toil. Yahweh scolded them:

> *Accursed be the soil because of you!*
> *Painfully will you get your food from it*
> *As long as you live.*
> *By the sweat of your face*
> *Will you earn your food,*
> *Until you return to the ground.*

Adam's curse was the curse of work. After the fall, creation would become, as Hopkins has it in a poem, "seared with trade; bleared, smeared with toil: / And wears man's smudge and shares man's smell." We've since lived in exile, dreaming of lost origins. One kind of dreaming that has fallen to artists and writers is the making of representations of that First Place.

The ascetic narrative in Genesis allows us to picture different Edens. The pedestrian version imagines the Garden as an emerald preserve, preternaturally becalmed, groomed like a tended plot, the beasts of the field benign and convivial like those in Edward Hicks's several versions of *Peaceable Kingdom*. But in a different dream, Eden is a prolix, overgrown tangle of vegetation, where animals of all sizes and temperaments—beetles, snakes, cows and crocodiles, lions and tigers, hummingbirds and hawks—go about their groaning and growling and twittering business. This Garden is a noisy, energetic stir where ripe fruit falls and leaves turn to meal, but where cycles of decay, death, and restoration are essential to the perfection and uniqueness of the place.

The Dutch photographer Ruud van Empel, born in 1958, came to prominence several years ago with photographs of children posed in lush green settings clearly meant to represent his own version of Eden: a picture perfect, maniacally tidy, mildly hallucinated diorama. Outsized or miniaturized dragonflies, beetles, birds, and grubs crawl upon or hover above plump spears of tall grass and supersize petals and fronds. All our mental images of the Garden are constructions, but van Empel's photographs don't simply remind us of that. They actually depict the mechanical process by which images are fabricated, because they're collages.

Photographic collage has been around since the beginning. Early image makers experimented with layering exposures. In 1858 the Englishman Henry Peach Robinson crafted a single image from five negatives that depicted a girl dying of consumption. Robinson bluntly stated his ethos. "Any 'dodge,' or trick, or conjuration of any kind," he wrote, "is open to the photographer's use so long as that it belongs to his art and is not false to nature." van Empel follows these axioms, but *his* images are photoshopped. Before it enters a photograph, every leaf blade, caterpillar, and dewdrop, every hand and nose and eye and pearl and glove and button, exists somewhere else. He selects visual facts, from his own photographs or scanned from other sources, then digitally glues them together. In his *World* series, where a Black child is posed in a dense garden of colossal spears of foliage, each element, down to the water beads on the heavily veined leaves, has been photo-shopped into the composite we see.

Van Empel's work is really about artificiality. He wants us to see the constructed nature of likeness or similitude. The imagery comes out of a surrealist matrix. Breton declared that surrealism combines two or more objects in order to create an object that never before existed. The enthralling, disturbing strangeness of the result—consider Meret Oppenheim's fur-covered cup, saucer, and spoon from 1936—is what surrealists meant by the Uncanny. Van Empel's inclination was evident quite early in his career. His mid-1990s *Office* series depicts executives seated confidently at desks surrounded by alarmingly odd objects (grotesquely outsized machine parts, precious cut stones, buttons constellated with other colorful millenary plenitude), and the black-and-white images in his 2002 *Photosketches* recall effects familiar from de Chirico, Magritte, and Man Ray: empty doorways, wedges of exaggerated light, slices of hard shadow, and unlikely objects (a chicken, a doll, a balloon, a manikin) all afloat in fuzzy atmospheres, induce a feeling of unreasonable foreboding.

Van Empel remains loyal to the Uncanny. In a recent image, the unnaturally angled head of a child perches on a clenched, bundled-up body, its features faintly smeared so that we can't quite bring into focus the face that's boldly staring right at us. In other photos, black-skinned children, set in what looks like a prefab Eden, shock us into recognizing our expectations about the whiteness of the human in the Garden. He knows he's unsettling us with the manipulated extremity of swampy greens and glassy blues in the enveloping vegetation; they starkly set off the blackness of the children's skin and the pop-out whites of their eyes. In his *Venus* series he wants us to see louche pop culture fused to high-art seriousness. Here, too, the subjects are Black girls whose languid postures imitate the slinky look of fashion models and also, just as convincingly, the sixteenth-century Lucas Cranach painting that inspired van Empel's version. His goddess, like Cranach's, wears a necklace, but the whiteness of the pearls jumps so hotly off the black skin that it carries a disconcertingly pleasurable erotic jolt.

This sort of art makes my jaws ache. It's self-aware to a stultifying fault. I find its weirdness and deadpan hyperspecificity contrived and airless. The landscapes in van Empel's *Theater* series present the natural order as a suffocating, manipulated environment. It's nature as a stage set, a fanatically tidy scene where only scripted events can take place. There's no wobble in this kind of locked-down art: the incipient surprise of chance doesn't stand a chance. Its subject is its own artificiality and the inherent manipulativeness of images of any kind, and it has a neutral, dulled-down affect. When the Black children in their Edens mildly pout, the photoshopped pout carries all the inauthenticity we might expect from the process that crafted it. Most of the figures in his work look like humanoid automata, none more so than a bashful self-portrait modeled after a dyspeptic 1912 painting by Otto Dix.

Van Empel's most compelling images, from the 2008 series *Souvenir*, were occasioned by the death of his mother. When he cleared out her house and found stuff associated with his childhood and family life, he photographed the objects then photoshopped and deployed the images to create homely, theatrical still lifes in which each item carries a tamped-down crackle of feeling. The concept and execution owe much to Joseph Cornell's shadow boxes, but the feeling tone has none of Cornell's whimsy, secrecy, and mystery. Van Empel wrote a short poem to accompany each image, and they have the same flat observational dispassionateness as the images; this works to his advantage, since the pictures are about how time estranges us (or not) from our experience. Here's the caption to a picture that offers up a juicer, mini-blender, colander, ladle and other things:

> *The plastic from the toothbrush holder has almost perished*
> *The chocolate box contains my school diplomas*
> *This could be our kitchen, in 1959*

All these original objects from that kitchen are not being used anymore
But they still exist.

The *Souvenir* series is more meditative than his other work and carries a shadowy melancholy. One image in particular charms and disarms. It displays the stuff of infancy: milk teeth in jewelry boxes, teething rings, a teddy missing one eye, a tarnished can of powder, and other things van Empel associates with his origins. He grew up in a traditional 1960s bourgeois Roman Catholic Dutch household, and these objects are, I think, the accoutrements of his own internalized Eden. They have (to quote Hopkins again) a "deep down freshness." In the poem that accompanies the image, van Empel writes:

The Babyderm container is still filled with baby powder
It smells good, even after 50 years.

2012

The Great War God

(Marsden Hartley)

In his 1950s poem, "Asphodel, that Greeny Flower," William
Carlos Williams describes a scene where he and a friend, "a distinguished artist," are standing on a train platform when a freight
train thunders through and kicks up dust. It's what Williams calls
"a picture of crude force." The friend says: "That's what we'd all
like to be, Bill." The artist is Marsden Hartley, born Edmund
Hartley in 1877 in Lewiston, Maine. In his twenties, Hartley left
Edmund behind and took his stepmother's surname. He studied
art first at the Cleveland Institute of Art after his family moved
to Ohio in 1892 then later at the National Academy of Design
in New York. By 1910 he was exhibiting at Alfred Stieglitz's 291
gallery and keeping company with other artists (Charles Demuth,
Paul Strand, John Marin, Edward Steichen) associated with the
gallery. He befriended writers and wrote poetry, criticism, and
autobiography. His early pictures are bold, romantic, declarative.
The best have the elegant blunt force Hartley admired in that
freight train, but this is the same artist who insisted on his spiritual
aspirations. To Stieglitz he wrote: "The essence which is in me is
American mysticism."

Many of Hartley's generation aspired to a freshly American
art, a feisty, smashing vernacular informed by European modern-
ism. In New York Hartley spent a lot of time in the studio of the
combustible visionary Albert Pinkham Ryder, who haunts the

landscapes Hartley made in his twenties. In 1912 he's on his way to Paris and in 1913 moves to Berlin, where he stays till 1916. He goes back to Europe in 1921 for several years but settles finally in Maine and becomes, like Cézanne, a local painter, a regionalist, and one of our greatest artists. In Berlin he befriended the sculptor Arnold Rönnebeck, who introduced him to his cousin, Karl von Freyburg. Hartley fell in love with von Freyburg, who was killed in the first months of World War I, and for several years his pictures mourned that loss. (Their recurrent triangular forms memorialize the three-pointed friendship the men shared.) The pictures made during his Berlin stay have the excitement that buzzed through German culture during the prewar years.

It's hard for us, knowing as we do the horrendous carnage WWI's newly mechanized warfare would deposit in history, to appreciate the enthusiasm so many felt for the onset of war. Even Rilke, whom so many now read as a gentle wisdom poet, announced in a poem the arrival of "the great war god" who would renew humanity. The raw unquestioned feverishness that must have been palpable in Berlin culture during the prewar years, a mix of artistic innovation, urban titillations, and military culture, was a kind of cohering irrationalism that wasn't, couldn't be, registered in consciousness in the moment. Hartley's German pictures express and are possessed by those energies. What he brought with him to Berlin wasn't just ambition, sexual desire, and an intense American appetite for European culture; he also brought a passion for the late nineteenth-century spiritual openness and vague raptures of Emerson and Whitman. Into this he folded European mystical traditions and the ambitions of painters like Kandinsky, Franz Marc, and Paul Klee to reveal in their work an invisible order of things. Mere geometries and colors were conduits to the unseen.

The act of painting and the images Hartley made were an expression of spiritual inquiry, even when the imagery is military. Martial flourish was spectacular in Wilhelmine Berlin, and Hartley had loved spectacle and splash since childhood, when the Barnum

& Bailey circus came through Lewiston. Every morning in Berlin a marching band and parade of guards trooped from the Brandenburg Gate to the Neue Wache (now the War Memorial), and Kaiser Wilhelm and his mounted troops often marched through the Tiergarten. Hartley's 1913 *Portrait of Berlin* floats in flattened space a festive assortment of consonant images: a Buddha housed in an almond-shaped shrine; a cuirassier and his mount enclosed in a circle, ramping on a mass of clouds whose shapes approximate the Buddha shrine; more cuirassiers (seen from behind as if on parade or marching off to war) and the Buddha contained in a triangle. Fastened onto this tight field are eight-pointed stars and the number 8, the stars an insignia of the regime, the digit a mystical symbol of regeneration that refers to a world beyond material reality.

I make it sound as if you need a visual glossary to understand the German pictures, and it does help to know how the signs and symbols relate to 1913 Berlin, but you don't need a key to be transported, as Hartley hoped, by the chalky whites edged in Prussian blues and the moody yellows that form a smudged aura around the charged objects and signs. You're inside Hartley's head and heart. Other pictures pick up other forms: rosettes, crosses, hieroglyphics, and musical staffs and clefs that assert Hartley's desire to make his painting a musical art, magical and suggestive and emotionally stunning as music is. He didn't really need the staffs and clefs. *The Warriors* may be the most beautiful and musically composed American picture about the rapture of military order. A mass of cuirassiers in shaggy-plumed Kaiser helmets are marching away, receding from us, while others bearing lances and standards parade across our field of vision. It's a strangely ecstatic song of yellows and reds, and the circular movement of the forms is rhapsodic, blending enthusiasm for military glamor with a faint overcast of dread for the destinies of those young men in such a fraught time.

When his spiritual feeling is too locked up in iconography,

Hartley's pictures can become ponderous and stiff. While in Germany he produced his so-called Indian pictures. Since the nineteenth-century Germans have had a genuine but most peculiar obsession with American Plains Indians. The best-selling German author ever is Karl May (200 million copies sold and still selling) who among other things wrote adventures set in a Wild West he never visited. Hartley's interest in Indian culture was mainly spiritual. It's unlikely he knew that Crazy Horse believed the material world to be a shadow world and that his spirit lived in another, truer reality, and so on shadow battlefields Crazy Horse was madly fearless, but *that's* the spiritual visionary-ness that appealed to Hartley. Pictures like *American Indian Symbols, Indian Composition,* and *Indian Fantasy,* with their tipis and canoes and eagles and suns and seated, pipe-smoking, noble redskins, are sclerotic and programmatic. They're interesting because they demonstrate that genuine feeling and authentic spiritual questing are no guarantee of good art.

In the more dire pictures following von Freyburg's death, Hartley's potent reds and blues and whites jolt from an unforgiving black ground. These elegiac paintings have an uneasy melancholic jubilance. Military vocabulary proliferates. One picture, *Painting No. 47, Berlin,* jams together helmet, parade bunting, sashes, regimental numbers, a boot spur, von Freyburg's initials, and the iron cross he was awarded. You can take your pleasure "reading" these paintings, but the wilder pleasure is induced by the explosive circulatory emotional and spiritual energies stirred up by the sheer pulse and rush of forms. A picture like *Portrait of a German Officer,* an extremely congested deployment of epaulets (Hartley all his life kept a pair of von Freyburg's silver epaulets), flagpole spearhead, lanyard, shoulder boards, cockades, a chessboard (von Freyburg loved the game), plus the numbers and flags and crosses and helmet decorations familiar from other pictures, induces in me an irrational lostness, not a stupor quite, but an emotional completeness that can't be reduced to a vocabulary of forms. Emily Dickinson's phrase for the effect I'm trying to convey, what the elegaic pictures really represent, is "a sumptuous destitution / —Without a name."

2014

Ripped

(Robert Mapplethorpe)

I was eleven or twelve when I befriended an older neighborhood boy who was a fanatical bodybuilder. Johnny pumped iron in the basement and would interrupt any conversation to do handstand pushups against a wall. He introduced me to bodybuilding competitions. I'd never seen anything like it, the modeling of the male body as sport and as what was not yet called performance art. The lights hardened and deepened the oiled musculature's cut: each competitor made himself into the trophy of his dreams. Johnny and I also paged through physique magazines that some of the grown-ups—this was the 1950s—might have considered male porn. It wasn't quite: the men wore briefer-than-briefs that outlined whatever you fantasized.

The theatricalized body idolatry in physique magazines was formative for the young Robert Mapplethorpe. Born in 1946 to middle-class parents in Queens, he aspired to be a famous artist but wasn't sure what kind. After high school he enrolled in the Pratt Institute in Brooklyn, joined ROTC, and majored first in advertising then in graphic arts. He dropped out before graduating and moved to New York, where he met Patti Smith (at first lover then lifelong friend) and people in Andy Warhol's circle. He made jewelry, collages, drawings, and mixed media constructions. By the mid-1970s gay male iconography was his favored, sometimes polemical, subject. In several early pieces on view in *Robert Map-*

plethorpe: The Perfect Medium, soft-core male magazine images are locked behind netting or boxed in or otherwise "censured." But by the late 1970s Mapplethorpe was making high-finish frontal images of nude males and not-quite-documentarian photographs of fetish and S / M activities in the leather clubs where he played and picked up boys who sometimes became his models.

Mapplethorpe was a fashion photographer whose couture was skin, mostly male, usually Black. When he died in 1989 he was the most incendiary high-toned image-maker in America and his photographs were blue chip acquisitions. Just after his death, The Corcoran Gallery in Washington, D.C., under pressure from Jesse Helms and other centurions of public morality, cancelled a traveling exhibit of his work: one *Self-Portrait* showed him in the famous hee-haw pose, his back to the camera with a bullwhip up his ass; another showed in extreme close-up a man inserting his pinky finger into his urethra. When the exhibition went to Cincinnati, antipornography militants charged the Contemporary Arts Center there with obscenity. (The CAC was acquitted.) At most venues, that exhibition, with its "X Portfolio" section off-limits to minors and firewalled with warnings to adults, drew crowds, not just because of the raree-show allure of guys double-fisting and weighting their scrotums with chains, but because it was an unsavory clandestine subculture elevated to officially fine-art status. (A lot of viewers assumed he was a rough guy, though friends of mine who knew him report a quiet, rather sweet person.) That wasn't the only stream in Mapplethorpe's work, but it was the one where his personal life, business smarts, and aesthetic canniness blended. He knew how to balance the elite satisfactions of elegant compositional strategies against the bad-boy swagger of swinging a dick in somebody's face.

Mapplethorpe once said that his work "moves toward a kind of perfection—it's just a matter of refining." He was raised Catholic, and the structured asceticism of ritual observance became in his art an austere perfectionism, whether he was depicting a

Corot-like spray of baby's breath, a black penis exposed through the open zipper of a polyester suit, a Pop close-up of a dollar bill, or one guy rimming another. There are altars all over the very early work, and the worshipful character of his sensibility (which fashion photographers cultivate) stayed with him. The work is adorational but so formally rigorous that the unruly passion adoration can stir up was contained by the sealed-lab environment of the frame. Aesthetic perfectionism in service to the perfectionism of the body didn't allow much ambiguity. I suspect his ambitions were conflicted: he may have aspired to a chancier wildness, but his sensibility (and awareness of what would sell) wouldn't allow it. A construction he made in 1971 is a kind of self-portrait: it's a cylinder filled with dice and fringed with a couple of rabbit feet, unlikely forms for an admitted control freak, but those dice are in a cage and the rabbit's feet are tied down.

In 1971, the 25-year-old Mapplethorpe met the 50-year-old collector Sam Wagstaff, who became lover and mentor to the young artist. Wagstaff gave Mapplethorpe a Polaroid camera, soon replaced by a Hasselbad, and urged him toward a more refined practice. The Polaroids' casual, hang-dog sincerity have the easy intimacy and coy look-at-me sultriness of family album images. Soon Mapplethorpe was expressing a different intimacy. He began to photograph skin in a way that was sensuously close *and* chillingly observational. He made the act of photography itself an act of costuming. Photography for him was idolatry that didn't try to coax unpredictable responses from the cult object. A "rubberman" (an S / M devotee packaged entirely in black leather) or a Black man in loin cloth and "tribal" face paint or a male nude perched on a pedestal only needs to present himself, like any still life object.

The images are driven by confessional impulses: Mapplethorpe wanted his images to possess the exquisiteness of the extremes he experienced in life; he wanted to give a masterpiece aura to things that pleasured him. He did this also by making portraits, most of them drained of personality, though a few are extraordinary. His picture of Deborah Harry is a masterpiece of dissolute beauty, and his many images of the bodybuilder Lisa Lyons are pieces of a life that seems driven by self-definition of every kind, whether she's hitting a muscle pose, dressing up as a languid pre-Raphaelite beauty, or acting the society babe in a flying saucer hat.

By the 1980s Mapplethorpe was photographing mostly the Black male body. These pictures more than any others express skin as costuming. The black penis was beautiful and part of the comprehensiveness of Mapplethorpe's essays on Black presence. For me, the extreme attention to muscle definition peaked by meticulous lighting and the ritualized self-awareness of the pose make many of these images too perfectly beautiful to be beautiful, except for one disquieting image that lets history flood in: a frontal shot of a naked Black man wearing a hood whose enfolded shape suggests both KKK costuming and the sheathed form of the man's penis.

Mapplethorpe's flower pictures are the favorites of many viewers, maybe because they're sexualized but in a well behaved, unthreatening way. They have the same norms of perfection, military precision, and priapic tenseness of the nudes, though a few have a more incipient, crouching motion, like a picture of tulips that lean into the frame like curious, probing birds. Some people are thrilled by Mapplethorpe's work. Some are not. I am not. Going through the exhibition I had to keep overriding boredom. The pictures' adventurous subject matter is usually sealed inside a picture-reality that refuses ambiguity, ambivalence, elusiveness, evanescence.

I'm criticizing Mapplethorpe for lacking what he probably didn't aspire to, but this indifference to interiority makes the work laborious, except for images where something springs loose, when the intensification of life that image-life compels jumps away from his control, like the Deborah Harry picture; or the double portrait of a couple bound and bandaged together top to bottom in gauze except for a gaping, plaintive, ecstatic mouth; or the portrait titled *Tim Scott*, whom we see in three-quarter profile combing his gelled ducktail, a rooster comb of stiff, glistening, jet hair arcing over his forehead: the musical staff faintly tattooed on his arm cuts tenderly across a heart.

2016

Exciting Events!

(Bill Traylor)

An artist can have innate skills and impeccable formal training and still not have what I think of as *strike*, the gift for making marks that have an arresting emotional and intellectual immediacy. Strike sets off a circulatory energy that runs through even the smallest detail or area of a picture. Scale doesn't matter. Neither does the style of the career. The painter Albert York (who died in 2009, at age 80) had strike: his small, homely landscapes and figure paintings throb. He lived and worked in Suffolk County, Long Island, a nonpresence in the New York art scene who worked slowly and didn't exhibit much. Jean-Michel Basquiat (who died in 1988, at age 28) had it, too. He went from musician to street tagger to glam-cool art star who made histrionic, fright-wig pictures with paint sticks. There's hipster bombast in Basquiat's work, but the art is real.

Basquiat was a street artist grabbing our attention even after he left the streets, and I don't know if he was aware of another, long-gone street artist and strike-meister, the African-American Bill Traylor. He might have been. Traylor had his first New York gallery solo show in 1980 and in 1982 was featured in an exhibition at the Corcoran Gallery in Washington, *Black Folk Art in America, 1930-1980*, that became a breakthrough moment for his reputation. He'd come a long way. Born into slavery sometime in the mid-1850s on an Alabama plantation, like many slaves he was given the planter's surname. After emancipation Traylor stayed on as a sharecropper until the late 1930s, when he moved to Montgomery and, for as long as his crippling rheumatism allowed, worked in a shoe factory. Thereafter he slept in the storage area of a funeral parlor or in a shoe repair shop and accepted whatever kindness came his way. It was then, roughly at age 85, that Traylor, who could not read or write, became a self-taught artist. He spent his days sitting outside the Pekin Colored Pool Room making drawings—over 1,400 of them—of the street life he observed, the memories he carried of his earlier farm life, and fantastical scenes that hooked observation to fantasy. He sold them to passersby for small change.

The sidewalks where Traylor sat and made his art were in Montgomery's Monroe Street neighborhood (aka "Dark Town"), a six-block district that in the 1930s and 1940s was a thriving center of African-American life, with a vivid street culture and Black-owned shops and businesses. (By 1980 it was gone, razed by developers.) Sometime in 1939, a young Montgomery-born artist named Charles Shannon introduced himself to Traylor, began buying his work, and over the next forty years became self-appointed conservator, archivist, and agent of Traylor's legacy. Shannon also kept notes of his conversations, so that we have Traylor's own occasional commentary on the drawings. Asked about a composition where madcap figures run around an architectural structure, Traylor told Shannon: "That's an exciting event," and so Traylor's multifigured pictures came to be referred to as Exciting Events. Shannon died in 1996 at age 81. Traylor died in 1949 at 95.

Peculiar pedestrians, pigs and mules and cows remembered from Traylor's sharecropper days, elephants he saw on Montgomery's streets in a circus parade, and fantastic creatures out of his imagination—Traylor's presentation of his subjects have a bold disingenuousness that carries a surge of enthusiastic feeling for what he sees. Each picture is a recording of the eye's encounter with the immediacy and fullness of the visual moment and has a voltage equal to the occasioning encounter. When figures aren't hurtling or climbing or falling, they're poised to do so. They're usually in some state of excitement or agitation, even street characters going about their ordinary business. One of these, a snappy, cakewalking gentleman in blue pants and plug hat, greets the world with his pipe and a pointed dagger-ish finger. Traylor drew with graphite, crayon, charcoal and—after Shannon brought him some—poster paint; he used different kinds of cardboard (boxes, shirt folders, the backs of advertising signs) sometimes stained and crudely ripped around the edges. There's no depth of field: Traylor drew his figures as like-sized pieces that might be moved around. Spatially every component shares the same plane. If he wanted to depict one figure passing another, he positioned it higher than the other. In one especially alarmed Exciting Event, we recognize a couple of beefy animal forms along with a guy with a rifle, a child clinging to the dress of his terrified mother, and a dipsomaniac shooting through the air in a hurdler's split. When Shannon asked what was going on, Traylor said: "Bear / bulldog / cat! Mens going to shoot bear. Everybody runs." Don't ask where Traylor might have seen a bear hunt in Montgomery or back on the plantation. His more fantastical pictures take bits of the present and other times and places and jiggers them together in hectic arrangements.

He loved street life: of his terrific picture of a couple squaring off, Traylor told Shannon, "She's not asking him where he's been, she's telling him." His street folk are galvanized in their particular picture space, quarreling, imbibing, standing with dainty pocketbook in hand, or spoiling for trouble: he referred to one picture of a guy angrily hopping up and down as *Fighter* because "he runnin' aroun' wantin' to fight." The men-women configurations can get ambiguous: we can't quite tell if they're happily cavorting or happily beating each other up. (Dogs and cats do the same.) And he loved the architectural forms of the Monroe Street neighborhood. A motif that looks like a tiered seafood tray derives from a fountain in Court Square, the liveliest public space thereabouts. Other geometric housings are based on a large, stout, four-faced public clock in the Square and the dome of the capitol building. In one image he recalls a swimming platform he and friends jerrybuilt long ago in the country: the picture, constructed out of elemental boxes and curves, catches the sensation of a memory momentarily occupied and lived again.

The drawings look stripped-down yet richly dense: Traylor relied on basic geometric forms that he filled in with crayon or paint or colored pencil. The coloring gives the figures an airy sensuousness. He had his own formal shorthand. Human torsos are boxy, like placards, printed with whatever the shirt or jacket or dress pattern might be. The guy whose woman is giving him a hard time sports a placket with four pert black buttons. One woman, hook-nosed like most of Traylor's figures, carries a handbag, her skirt a trapezoid, her green-blouse torso a square, and capping all this is an umbrella modeled on the capitol dome.

Some Exciting Events are Traylor's reworking of church-meeting configurations of preacher and congregants, or anecdotal scenes like the one of a hatchet-wielding lady chasing a turkey. There's also a fair amount of public boozing on display. One tipsy gentleman knocks back his half-pint while balancing on a dainty, uplifted foot. The bigger fun for us, though, is following the artist's hand as it roughs out the figure's outline then fills in the physique with swirling, mottled sepia marks that are a gestural imagining of skeleton and muscle. Traylor liked to pose figures, even sober ones, at a tipping point, barely holding their balance on quarter-moon legs pegged daintily to the ground. The figures perched on platforms, hovering like raucous angels, or pitching down with zippy speed, have an antic grace, spirited and angular, a little lost but game for life, holding on to their tiny purchase.

Intending to help Traylor upgrade or "professionalize" his materials, Shannon gave him fresh, store-bought poster board, but he didn't like it. He preferred distressed surfaces fatigued with use, and he sometimes played with the irregularly shaped cardboard signs he scavenged from the trash or found on sidewalks; a torn, rounded edge will rhyme, say, with the shape of a bull's horns or a mule's torso. Traylor's stark, excited energy thins out in the late pictures. He spent his last years traveling to visit his scattered children in Philadelphia, Detroit, and elsewhere, and his health was failing. (He lost a leg to diabetes.) But the drawings he made in his prime are tight little songs of praise. One of my favorites depicts a slinky elongated rabbit running across its improvised space. Like so much of Traylor's work, it's blunt, radical, and quickened with comic grace.

2013

Postscript

Notes on Prose and Poetry

Poetry is saturated with origins—one's personal origins, the originating occasion of a poem, species origins, and all the experiences that are life's ongoing articulations and elaborations of origins. I think of prose as the study and analysis of origins, genealogies, all the lines of descent that I try to ravel into sentences that, when the work is going well, surprise me, as if they're dancing without my instruction or assistance. Poetry gives voice to origins—aggrieved, ecstatic, inquiring voice. Certain books like Claude Lévi-Strauss's *Tristes Tropiques* and Cesare Pavese's *Dialogues with Leucò*. Both are spiritual autobiographies; they're also investigations into the origins of consciousness, into mythic thinking, social convention, and human behavior.

◉◉◉

The need to express is different from the need to talk about something. For me, poetry is pressured, *struck*, into existence. It comes more directly and chaotically off my nerves than critical or reflective prose, even when a poem's subject is deliberation. It's the drama of deliberation, the insistence of it, that matters most. Prose exposes or X-rays or scans the process of deliberation, and it requires a judiciousness that lyric poetry doesn't want or need.

◎◎◎

Christopher Marlowe's murder was occasioned by a "reckoning," a bar tab. A reckoning of any kind is a sort of counting up, a summing or squaring off of things. It's purposeful, methodical, plotted. Poetry isn't purposeful like that. It's messier and formally more plastic. It bears the smells and textures, bricky or loamy, of the vaguest reaches of soul life. The more crystalline it becomes, the more fraught with ambiguity; it has a punchier and more elegant immediacy than prose. Its engine isn't reckoning but recognition, an impassioned greeting that comes out of the mash of subjectivity. Reflective prose thrives on the appearance of objectivity, except when the writer is Emerson, Leopardi, Nietzsche, Cioran, William James, master interrogators of the nature of illusion.

◎◎◎

"Essay" has embedded in it "assay," "weighing," "testing," "proofing," "trying out," "attempting." When writing prose I'm arguing mostly with myself and the friends and predecessors whose voices are in my head. Essaying is always an act of criticism. Autobiography, too, is a criticism of life, criticism as an ongoing assessment of value. If I'm writing about literary things or the visual arts, I'm also arguing with aesthetic facts, with texts or images, or with other poets and critics. It's explanatory and demonstrative and exemplifying. Great essaying critics like Dr. Johnson, Coleridge, Pater, and Erich Auerbach, have a sense of personal destiny, theirs, folded into the shapely immediacy of their prose. And they wrote with the destiny of the race in view. They instruct incidentally (and greatly), but they aren't really interested in instructing.

◎◎◎

Poetry is revelation. It cracks open the things of the world. It has a terrible freshness. It still hangs close by its religious and ritualistic origins. It has a household grandeur and universal obsessions: it notices and restores to consciousness a caterpillar on a leaf or the limitless ways of human violence and conflict. But its primary purpose is revelation, first-order revelation, naked, unexplained, exasperatingly real. Writing critical prose is an act of thinking about revelation, the preparatory self stuff. Prose writing primes the poetic imagination.

◉◉◉

Writing poetry is animal activity. It demands things of me. It can have a terrible neediness. It maintains its own wild nature even while being shaped by the pattern-giving imagination. Prose makes no such demands. Its pressures are more intellectual than sensational. It's more social, normalized, negotiated by and for the inquisitive self. Its expressive imperatives are different from those that drive poetry. Something has been or is being thought through, worked over, concluded from. The news we get from critical prose doesn't stay news the way poetry does, though in both practices freshness is everything. Poetry, lyric poetry at least, the kind of lyricism I love in poets like Lorine Niedecker and W. S. Graham, lives much of its life in the kingdom of essences. So much of poetry is about inconstancy, change, transformations, instability, fear, fury. It's a release, an abandonment, while prose is a gesture of containment, a proofing of experience, not an all-but-raw, red, granular expression of it.

◉◉◉

Prose gives me the formal spaciousness to pick something up, examine it, fool with it, show it to friends and strangers, then put it away, tear it up, or publish it. It's all content, even when I have a musical feeling for what's happening. One pleasure of writing prose is the canny shaping of content and the emotion content stirs in me. Poetry's purpose is to cry out, to cry in good faith and with a passion that takes the shape of the cry and only happens that once. A poem gives meaningful shape to the content of the cry that a poem is.

◎◎◎

Prose has a formal spaciousness and operates in an interrogative mood. It's saner than poetry, and those who think that poetry's derangements are a corrupt or juvenile or self-dramatizing belief are welcome to their measured rationalism. The orders of poetry clarify, enhance, and preserve the disorders of experience. There are voices at my shoulder when I'm writing poems; when I write prose I'm talking *back* at those voices. Few intellectual pleasures match the satisfaction of becoming lost or disoriented in a passage of prose and trying to understand, in the process of writing, how I got there, then finally finding my way out. Prose is the act of writing toward an understanding. I don't write poetry to find understanding, or map out its process: understanding is beside the point—the point being expressiveness, the stretched sustained appeal or prayer or shout that a poem can be. Poetry is an act of beseeching, even when it's asking for nothing at all: it *presents* as beseeching. I ask of my poems, "What do you want of me, from me?" or "Leave me alone a moment" or "What can *I* offer *you*?" Poetry asks the same of me. It's an entity greater than my own minor being. Prose marks or draws or narrates the extension and limits of my being. Of the two, prose is a better citizen.